The Do-It-Yourself Accounts Payable Consultant Handbook (3rd Edition)

Mary S. Schaeffer
Accounts Payable Now & Tomorrow

Third Edition
Some of this material appeared originally in the
Accounts Payable Now & Tomorrow
newsletter

www.ap-now.com
560 Peoples Plaza #197 Newark DE 19702
For information about reprints, the newsletter or other matters, contact
Publisher@ap-now.com or call 302 836 0540

Table of Contents

Table of Contents

Table of Contents

Introduction

No one knows your organization better than you do. That's why you are in the best position to make process improvements for your own operations. But, sometimes you are too close to identify those problem spots that have crept into your procedures. That's where The DIY Accounts Payable Consultant Handbook comes in. It provides you the added perspective to see your operation clearly. It effectively lets you take that giant step back so you can look at your accounts payable function objectively.

Use our straightforward problem-solving tools to uncover the weak spots in your processes. Once you've identified the problems our commentary will get you started on the right path to fixing the problem by providing some best practice advice. You can use this to strengthen your controls preventing duplicate and erroneous payments and fraud. What's more, you might even earn a few more early pay discounts.

Each section contains:

- Several analytical checklists to help you scrutinize the your processes to identify those areas that need attention; (with Blue headers)
- An explanation of why certain practices are not recommended and others are (with dark red headers): and
- The latest thinking to help you develop the solution that is right for your operations (with green headers).

The diagnostics are tricky. Don't be lulled into thinking you know the correct answers. For a few of the checklists, the correct answer is the same for every question, i.e. if you are doing things correctly the correct answer will always be Yes. However, several of the lists have one or two items where the correct answer does not follow the pattern, so pay close attention as you work your way through the diagnostics.

The book is laid out so you can photocopy the checklists for use by several members of your staff. Have two or more associates complete the checklists to see if you agree on your current processes and the direction you should take the department.

Don't expect to hit 100%. Almost without exception, no organization does. Sometimes there are industry issues that prevent complete compliance and other times it is simply a matter of corporate culture, a senior management reluctance or lack of time and/or money to implement the changes.

The best practice advice offered at the end of each section is not meant to be comprehensive but rather as a starting point to get the reader on the right path. **DIYAP**

Invoices

- Invoice Handling Diagnostic
- Invoice Processing Diagnostic
- Do Your Processors Know the Basics
- Convincing Vendors to Invoice Electronically
- Best Practice Advice: Five Best Practices to Eliminate Invoice Headaches
- Best Practice Advice: Are Paper Invoices *Really* Necessary?
- Best Practice Advice: How Four Companies Gain Efficiency Using E-mail/Fax to Receive Invoices

Invoice Handling Diagnostic

Invoice handling is the backbone of all accounts payable operations. While on the face of it, handling invoices shouldn't be that complicated, it's really easy to miss one little detail and make a real mess of the process. Let's see how your invoice handling stacks up.

1) Do you get copies of purchase orders and receiving reports directly from the issuing departments? ____Yes ____No

2) Do you compare invoice quantities, prices and terms with those on the purchase order? ____Yes ____No

3) Do you compare invoice quantities with those on the receiving report? ____Yes ____No

4) When you receive a typed invoice (rather than one that is computer generated) do you check the accuracy of the calculations? ____Yes ____No

5) Do you pay invoices on time so as to avail the organization of all available discounts? ____Yes ____No

6) Do you receive all invoices from vendors in a central location, ideally the accounts payable department? ____Yes ____No

7) In addition to a centralized mailing address, do you proved an email address and fax number where vendors can send invoices should they choose to deliver them that way? ____Yes ____No

8) Do your procedures ensure the accounts payable system is properly accounting for unmatched receiving reports and invoices? ____Yes ____No

9)Do you regularly compare monthly vendor statements with accounts payable balances?

____Yes ____No

10)Do you restrict access to the master vendor file to employees authorized to make changes and set up new vendors?
____Yes ____No

11)Do employees who make changes to the master vendor file also process invoices or handle payments? ____Yes ____No

12)Do you have a process for tracking invoices received before releasing them for departmental approval and/or other processing? ____Yes ____No

13)Do you have a process for reviewing the approvals of invoices (vouchers) for completeness of supporting documents? ____Yes ____No

14)If an invoice is received from a supplier not previously dealt with, do you have a process for ascertaining that the supplier actually exists? ____Yes ____No

15)Do you have a process for assigning responsibility for ensuring all cash discounts are taken and if, applicable, exemptions from sales, federal excise, and other taxes are claimed? ____Yes ____No

16)Do you have a process for referring differences in invoice and purchase order price, terms, shipping arrangements or quantities to the purchasing department for review and approval? ____Yes ____No

17)Do you have a process for notifying accounts payable and purchasing departments of returned purchases so those purchases can be matched with vendor advices?
____Yes ____No

18)Do you have a process for assigning responsibility for ensuring all exemptions from sales, federal excise, and other taxes are claimed? ____Yes ____No

Explanation of the Best Practice Responses

We hope you didn't fall into the trap thinking all the answers to the questions were the same this time. One question has a different answer. Did you figure out which one?

Obviously, the correct answer for most of the questions is a resounding Yes. However, the correct answer for question #11 is No. Proper segregation of duties is critical for any organization that is concerned about best practices and strong internal controls.

Having the same employee process invoices and make changes to the master vendor file violates the basic segregation of duties principles. By not allowing the same person to handle both tasks, the problem of employees playing games with the master vendor files is eliminated. **DIYAP**

The Invoice Processing Diagnostic

The key to paying an invoice only once is in the processing of an invoice once it gets to the accounts payable department. This seemingly innocuous process is loaded with places where mistakes can be made. Worse, weak processes make it easy so those with a little knowledge and sticky fingers can lighten your company's bank account of funds they are not entitled to. This diagnostic will help you zero in those potential weak links in your current system.

1) Do you sometimes insert a letter in the front of an invoice number to "force" a payment through your system? ____ Yes ____ No

Potential Issue: This one has duplicate payment written all over it. Many companies have duplicate payment routines that they run before payments are released. These typically key off the invoice number. The leading indicator that was added will slide through the program without raising a flag every time.

2) Do you have an invoice numbering standard that results in a unique numeric to assign invoice numbers to invoices without invoice numbers? ____ Yes ____ No

Potential Issue: Without the unique identifier, invoices can end up being paid two or more times. Some companies create an invoice number based on the date and some other feature. This can result in numerous duplicate invoice numbers and makes it impossible to easily identify a potential duplicate payment.

3) Do you have a stringent process that you go through before paying a copy or duplicate invoice? ____ Yes ____ No

Potential Issue: Paying for copies or faxes is one of the leading ways a duplicate payment occurs. Often the initial payment is made from the copy and then a second payment is made when the original finally winds its way down to the accounts payable department. This is more likely to happen in organizations where there are not strict controls on the timing of the approval process and/or vendors are not given clear instructions on where to send an invoice for payment.

4) Are your vendors given clear instructions on where to direct invoices for payment? ____ Yes ____ No

Potential Issue: Without clear instructions invoices sometimes take a bit longer than would be expected to end up in accounts payable. They may go to several different departments before ending up to be processed. This can result in the vendor sending a second invoice, which only increases the chance of a duplicate payment being made.

5) Do you have a process for escalating the approval of an invoice if the original approver is unavailable (or simply neglects to address the issue)? ____ Yes ____ No

Potential Issue: While most approvers are quite good about reviewing invoices for approval and returning them to accounts payable for payment, a few tardy individuals can throw a cog into the entire process. Additionally, if there is no mechanism in place to handle approvals when the approver is on vacation or is out unexpectedly, further delays will be introduced into the process. These delays increase the likelihood that the vendor will send a second invoice, which, as you know, increases the odds of a second payment.

6) Do you have a standard for your processors to use when entering invoice numbers?
_____ Yes _____ No

Potential Issue: If you don't have an agreement on the way leading zeros, dashes within numbers and similar matters are handled, your processors will each develop their own inconsistent methodology for entering invoice numbers. The results will allow duplicate invoice numbers to slip through your duplicate payment checking routines.

7) Do you have a standard naming process to be used when entering information into the Master Vendor File? _____ Yes _____ No

Potential Issue: If you don't have a standard you will end up with duplicate entries in the master vendor file for the same vendor. This is an open invitation for both duplicate payments and fraud.

8) Is the same standard naming process used by those responsible for the Master Vendor file used by your processors when processing invoices? _____ Yes _____ No

Potential Issue: If you don't have an agreement on how numbers in names, the word the at the beginning of a name and other such issues are handled, you will end up with your processors entering vendor names differently than the person who sets the vendors up in the master vendor file. You will end up with mismatches galore increasing the work in the department.

9) Have you segregated the responsibility for processing invoices from approving invoices?
_____ Yes _____ No

Potential Issue: Without the proper segregation of duties, collusion will not be needed to perpetrate a fraud. This lack makes it easier for an individual to submit a phony invoice and get it approved for payment, increasing the likelihood of employee and/or vendor fraud.

10) Have you segregated the responsibility for processing invoices from entering information into the master vendor file? _____ Yes _____ No

Potential Issue: By not segregating these two tasks properly it becomes easy for a crooked employee to divert a legitimate payment to a fraudulent account. Fraud increases any time duties are not appropriately segregated.

11) Have you segregated the responsibility for approving invoices for payments from entering data into the master vendor file? _____ Yes _____ No

Potential Issue: Once again, without the proper separation it becomes much simpler for an employee to submit a phony invoice and have it approved. The chances of experiencing a fraud increase when these responsibilities are not properly segregated.

12) Does someone in upper management review a report of all changes made to the Master Vendor File? _____ Yes _____ No

Potential Issue: This review, however boring, is a front line defense against employee fraud through manipulation of the master vendor file. Sometimes just knowing the entries will be closely reviewed and scrutinized is enough to keep a larcenous employee from playing games with the master vendor file.

Explanation of Best Practice Responses

As you may have gathered, the ideal answer to all these questions is "Yes," with the exception of the first question, where the ideal is "No." If you've answered otherwise, go back and review the processes in question. You have a gap in your internal controls that could permit a duplicate payment, fraud or both. Take the appropriate steps to close that loophole. **DIYAP**

Don't Get Tripped Up on The Basics: A Best Practice Quiz for Your Processor

Is your staff up to speed on the basics or do they occasionally miss something? This month's checklist focuses on basic areas where a few processors sometimes fall down. Let your processors take the quiz. Their answers could indicate whether you need to do some additional training.

1. Do you lock your computer or sign out any time you leave your desk? ___ Yes ___ No
2. Do you take special care when entering the vendor's invoice number or just enter anything because you are more focused on the details important to your organization? ___ Yes ___ No
3. Do you search every invoice for indications that an early payment discount might be offered? ___ Yes ___ No
4. Do you look closely at invoices to make sure they don't say "paid by credit card" somewhere in small print? ___ Yes ___ No
5. Do you use the coding standards set up by your company for all information entered when processing invoices? ___ Yes ___ No
6. If you are not certain of how a piece of information should be entered when processing invoices, do you refer to the company's coding standards? ___ Yes ___ No
7. If you are not certain how a particular invoice should be processed do you ask or check the policy and procedures manual to make sure you have it right rather than guessing? ___ Yes ___ No
8. Do you keep track of your open disputed invoices and check with the people helping resolve the discrepancy every few days? ___ Yes ___ No
9. Are you careful about clicking on links and downloading attachments received via email? ___ Yes ___ No
10. Are you careful about clicking on links when checking your personal email on the company's computer? ___ Yes ___ No
11. If you suspect your computer has been infected with a virus or malware, do you immediately notify your supervisor? ___ Yes ___ No
12. If a vendor gets nasty on the phone, do you hold your temper and remain professional?

___ Yes ___ No

13. Do you return calls to vendors promptly? ___ Yes ___ No

14. When a vendor calls asking for a piece of information you need to research, do you get back to them within 48 hours, even if it is just to let them know you are still working on it? ___ Yes ___ No

15. When someone comes demanding a Rush check, do you automatically issue it? ___ Yes ___ No

16. Do you pay credits? ___ Yes ___ No

17. Do you occasionally share passwords with fellow processors when someone is taking vacation and you have to fill in? ___ Yes ___ No

18. When the system indicates the invoice number you are entering when processing an invoice is not acceptable as it has already been used, do you just add a space, dot or letter to the end of the invoice number to force it through? ___ Yes ___ No

19. Do you schedule invoices for immediate payment just to get them off your desk and out of your queue? ___ Yes ___ No

20. When you discover a way to change procedures to make the work process faster and/or more efficient, do you immediately implement it? ___ Yes ___ No

Answer Summary

Total Yes 1-14

Total No 15-20 __________

Total

Explanation of Best Practice Responses

Hopefully your total score on the quiz on the preceding pages was 20. That would indicate your processors are not making any little mistakes that could cost your organization. Let's take a look at the reasoning behind each response.

1. If you don't lock your computer or sign out any time you leave your desk you are opening the door to any thief walking by who could just slip into your cubicle and either access information they have no right to or worse. If you are enabled to make payments on behalf of your company, they could initiate a fraudulent payment. What's worse, is when the fraud unraveled it would appear as though the processor created those transactions. While this isn't likely to happen often, you only need one incident to create a disaster.

2. Effective processors realize that by taking special care when entering the vendor's invoice number they are increasing their chances of identifying a duplicate invoice and preventing a duplicate payment. Sometimes, processors are more focused on the details important to their organization not realizing how critical it is that the invoice number be entered correctly.

3. Early payment discounts are a gold mine for the companies receiving them. Vendors don't always reveal that they offer them. Processors who search every invoice for indications that an early payment discount might be offered are adding value to their organization.

4. One of the biggest causes of duplicate payments are invoices that are paid twice using two different payment vehicles. By looking closely at invoices to make sure they don't say "paid by credit card" somewhere in small print processors can help ensure their organization doesn't fall into that trap.

5. Strict coding standards represent the very best way to prevent duplicate payments. By adhering to the standard set up by the company for all information entered when processing invoices, processors can put a big dent in the number of duplicate payments made. In fact, some organizations have reported that a strict adherence to coding standards has eliminated a huge portion of their duplicate payments.

6. There is nothing wrong with referring coding standards when someone is not certain how a piece of information should be entered when processing invoices. In fact, it is a recommended best practice and a sure way to avoid mistakes.

7. Likewise, if you are not certain how a particular invoice should be processed asking or checking the policy and procedures manual to make sure you have it right is a recommended best practice. Guessing will eventually get you into trouble.

8. Tracking your open disputed invoices and checking with the people helping resolve the discrepancy every few days is one way to ensure no invoice gets lost in the process.

9. If you are careful about clicking on links and downloading attachments received via email, you will limit the chances of downloading malware onto your computer and inadvertently opening the organization up to ACH fraud.

10. Likewise, if you are careful about clicking on links when checking your personal email on the company's computer you will also help protect the organization against a malicious attack from a cyber-crook.

11. If you suspect your computer has been infected with a virus or malware, immediately notify your supervisor so IT can be contacted. They will send someone to scan your machine and take the proper steps to eliminate any problems.

12. When a vendor gets nasty on the phone, holding your temper and remaining professional is critical. Otherwise you could end up inflaming the situation. This is not always easy to do. End the call as quickly as possible and make your supervisor aware of the situation.

13. Returning calls to vendors promptly is a sign of the true professional and will go a long way towards cementing good relations with suppliers.

14. When a vendor calls asking for a piece of information you need to research, calling them back within 48 hours, even if it is just to let them know you are still working on it is another sign of a professional and one that cares about vendor relations.

15. When someone comes demanding a Rush check, don't automatically issue it. This will simply lead to more requests and more Rush checks. Question them about why they

need to Rush. Sometimes, they don't really need a check immediately and when you explain your normal process, it will meet their payment delivery needs. Of course, the best way to handle rush payment requests is to insist on ACH payments for all immediate demands. However, this is a policy decision that needs to be made at the managerial level.

16. Credits represent money owed the company not money the company owes the vendor. Instead of paying the credits, it should be used to reduce the payment on another invoice.

17. Sharing passwords with fellow processors when someone is taking vacation and you have to fill in is a bad practice. In fact, sharing passwords is never a good idea. Instead of creating a clear audit trail, it blurs the trail. Whenever you fill in for someone, you should be given your own password. Avoid the temptation to give someone your password when in a crush. It may be easier but it is a sign of weak controls.

18. When the system indicates the invoice number you are entering when processing an invoice is not acceptable as it has already been used, don't try and force the invoice through. The system is telling you it has been paid. Do some research. By adding a space, dot or letter to the end of the invoice number to force it through the odds are high you will be making a duplicate payment.

19. While a clean desk is great, it isn't such a good thing if you get it by paying vendors early. That costs your organization money which comes right off the bottom line. Scheduling invoices for immediate payment just to get them off your desk and out of your queue is a bad practice and one that should be eliminated from your repertoire.

20. When you discover a way to change procedures to make the work process faster and/or more efficient, the proper approach is to discuss it with your supervisor. It may work in accounts payable but create more work for another department. If it is a good recommendation, it should be implemented by all processors. Otherwise an inconsistent approach could end up in duplicate payments. Let your manager make the call. That is their job.

So how'd your processors do? If more than one or two of your processors answered the same question incorrectly it might be time for some additional training. **DIYAP**

Convincing Vendors to Invoice Electronically

Are you still dealing with piles of paper invoices? Do you know that e-invoicing, even if it only means vendors are e-mailing invoices, is a better way to go but you can't seem to get your suppliers to agree? Look over AP Now's e-Invoicing Benefits Checklist below to make sure you've pointed out every last benefit to your reluctant suppliers.

1. Have you pointed out to your suppliers that faster receipt of invoices means it is more likely you'll have the invoiced processed in time to pay on the due date? __ Yes __ No

2. Have you pointed out the cost savings associated with not having to print invoices? __ Yes __ No

3. Have you pointed out the cost savings associated with not having to pay for postage? __ Yes __ No

4. Have you pointed out the cost savings related to salaries of associates who won't have

to manually stuff of invoices in envelopes? __ Yes __ No

5. Have you pointed that no longer will invoices be lost in the mail? __ Yes __ No

6. Have you pointed out that should the vendor lose an invoice, replacing it will be simple and inexpensive? __ Yes __ No

7. Have you reminded your suppliers that with e-invoicing there's no need to take invoices to post office? __ Yes __ No

8. Have you suggested that in the unlikely event they had to send second invoices if a customer (not you, of course) hadn't paid by due date, the process is much simpler than in a paper based environment? __ Yes __ No

9. Have you reminded your suppliers that if and e-mail address is not good, they would be notified immediately, not two to eight weeks later when mailed invoices finally come back? __ Yes __ No

10. Have you also noted that invoices don't get damaged in the e-mail the way they occasionally do in snail mail? __ Yes __ No

Discussion of AP Now's e-Invoicing Benefits Checklist

We don't think it necessary to go through each of the items on the checklist in individual detail. We think the responses are obvious. All of the items on the checklist are benefits to the supplier sending invoices. Clearly, there are also a whole slew of benefits to the customer, as well. But the purpose of the checklist is to arm organizations who are trying to convince vendors to bill electronically so the focus is on that end only. That is why we don't discuss things like making it easier to earn early payment discounts.

That's a clear benefit to the customer and with interest rates as low as they are, many vendors would like to eliminate them completely. So, it is better not to mention them when trying to convince suppliers to start billing electronically. There is one exception. If you have a supplier strapped for cash who is often pushing to get paid earlier and it offers an early-pay discount, then by all means, mention that as a factor when trying to convince that vendor to bill electronically.

It should be noted that while the biggest return is an automation of the whole process, this is not an all or nothing proposition. If the only change you can make is to get vendors to send invoices by e-mail, that is a big step in the right direction and don't dismiss it. Grab it. Many of today's third party invoice automation models have the ability to accept invoices sent by e-mail.

If you can't convince a particular vendor to convert, don't give up. Periodically go back to them to see if they've changed their position. While you may not be a big enough customer to make them see things your way, another customer might. And, once they start doing it for one, they are likely to see the benefits and be more than willing to do it for your organization as well. **DIYAP**

Best Practice Advice: 5 Practices to Eliminate Invoice Headaches

There's an old adage in the accounts payable world that "a good invoice gets a good and timely payment." Ah, if only it were that simple. And if we are going to be totally honest, we'd have to acknowledge that submitting an accurate invoice is only part of the equation. The invoice has to get where it belongs before it can be processed in a timely manner. Now, if you're reading this thinking that good invoice preparation has nothing to do with accounts payable, you are mistaken. Accounts payable, with management's support, can play a large part in putting an end to the nightmares caused by invoices. Let's take a look at some of the problems along with solutions to minimize them.

1) **Invoices addressed to no one.** Every organization gets them. Addressed to no one, it floats from department to department waiting for someone to adopt and approve it. Many organizations are reluctant to return these invoices to their vendors for further clarification for fear of offending them. But that's exactly what they do when the invoice can't be easily identified and, as a result, ends up being paid late. We believe a better approach is to draft a polite form letter informing vendors that in order to be paid in a timely manner, they should provide either the name of the person who authorized the purchase and/or a legitimate PO number. A copy of this form letter should be attached to every unidentified invoice and immediately sent back to the vendor.

2) **Invoices arrive in accounts payable after the due date.** This is an old problem faced by many accounts payable departments. It usually results in finger pointing between accounts payable and purchasing. A much simpler approach is to have all invoices go to accounts payable *first*. Then, accounts payable can scan and e-mail invoices out for approval. The beauty of this approach is it eliminates mail time and there is an audit trail of who sent what when. Even if the scanning option is not available, by having the information logged into accounts payable first, it puts accounts payable in a better position to respond to vendor inquiries.

3) **Small low-dollar invoices with no purchaser name.** Sometimes the dollar amount on invoices doesn't seem to warrant a serious investigation. If there is no purchaser name or company PO number, return the invoice as you would an invoice addressed to no one requesting additional information. Yes, this takes valuable time away from other value-added tasks, but many of these invoices are scams and you don't want your people paying them. Once you pay one of these fraudulent invoices you will definitely receive more of them.

4) **Invoices not reflecting special deals.** This is an age-old problem. Purchasing negotiates a great special deal; it could be extended payment terms or a new, low price good for a limited amount of time. If the PO is not filled out including this information, accounts payable will pay according to the standard terms/pricing. It's a fact of life that vendors "forget" to reflect special arrangements on the invoice. This happens all the time. In one organization, invoices that were supposed to be paid in 120 days were paid in 10. That's a serious loss to the organization that paid early. Make it company policy that all POs are filled out completely.

5) **Invoices delayed in the mail so the early payment discount is lost.** Occasionally invoices do get lost in the mail but it is amazing how often this happens with large invoices offering early payment discounts. In one case, it wasn't that the invoice was lost in the mail but rather the vendor was pulling them for review before sending because of the dollar amount involved. While the intent wasn't to deny the discount, the end result was the same. If you suspect a vendor is playing games, save the envelopes showing the postmark date. An even better solution is to move to electronic invoicing so the mail time goes to zero. This can be a formal electronic invoicing program or the vendor simply e-

mailing the invoice. Another approach taken by some organizations is to mark these invoices for special faster processing. Whatever approach you take, the desired outcome is to get the invoices with early payment discount opportunities quickly. **DIYAP**

Best Practice Advice: Are Paper Invoices Really Necessary?

A note arrived in our in-box the other day from one of our readers. "Can vendors demand we accept only e-mail or fax invoices?" it asked. This piqued our interest so we started investigating and found that the way all sorts of organizations receive invoices is being turned on its head. What's more, as our investigation continued, we discovered something intriguing: many accounts payable departments are receiving invoices either by e-mail or fax rather than through the mail. In fact, many are encouraging vendors to send them in this manner. And a good number of those who haven't explored that avenue think it's a great idea. What follows is an in-depth look at this issue with advice on how you can take advantage of this growing phenomenon.

Death of the Sacred Cow

Do you remember when one of the best ways to prevent a duplicate payment was to never pay from a fax or copy of an invoice? Paying only from the original invoice was deemed to be a good control. Well, it still would be except for one thing. As many readers noted, with technology, there is no such thing as one original invoice. You can have as many originals as you like—and they all look great!

Given that sad reality, there is no reason to insist on only paying from an original invoice; that control simply doesn't work anymore. Not only that, but by refusing to accept faxed invoices, organizations are bypassing a great tool that will help them get invoices faster—and thus enable them to earn more early payment discounts.

Trend

Certain big organizations have made this issue part of their terms and conditions. "If you want to do business with us you have to agree to accept your invoice electronically," they insist. Expect to see more of this as time goes on.

A growing number of organizations see the benefits, which we'll examine more closely in a minute, and now encourage invoices by e-mail and fax. And some actually prefer fax. No, you are not seeing things. The reason they prefer fax is that they direct the fax to an e-fax number that reads right into their imaging system actually making their life a little easier. *Accounts Payable Now & Tomorrow* expects this trend to pick up speed and within a few short years, paper invoices will be the rarity rather than the norm. If you haven't adjusted your processes to include receipt of invoices by both e-mail and fax, you might want to consider making the change.

Just when You Think You've Heard Everything

Quite a few organizations have been told that their vendors won't be sending paper invoices in the future. One company shared with us that they have had vendors take this one step further and tell them the vendor intended to charge for issuing paper invoices. We don't really expect this to become a popular tactic, although we do predict that a few of the 800-pound gorillas will use this approach to force acceptance by their smaller customers.

With the low cost of technology today, money should not stand in the way of any organization adopting the e-mail/fax invoice acceptance methodology. If for some reason, one of the approaches is not palatable, we've not seen any vendor insisting on all fax or all e-mail so there is really no reason not to join this revolution.

Benefits to the Fax/e-Mail Methodology

The advantages to the vendor are clear: no postage, paper, or printing costs. But, does the recipient benefit? Although the advantages to the customer are not as clear cut, they are considerable, nonetheless. Here's a partial list of why you should consider the e-mail/fax approach.

- No envelopes to open; better use of staff time.
- No invoices lost in the mail.
- No time delays.
- Easier to earn early payment discounts.
- Disputes/questions handled by replying to the original e-mail.
- Can upload e-faxed invoices into system.

Drawbacks

Interestingly, we only found our readers reacting adversely in a few cases. Their objections were as follows:

- E-mail requires printing out invoices.
- Must ensure the fax tray has paper.
- Must ensure the invoice was delivered to AP and not elsewhere in the case of a shared fax.
- Large volume vendors necessitate a lot of printing help.
- Illegible fax printing makes processing the invoice difficult.

While we can see the validity in these objections, they can be overcome fairly easily.

What Accounts Payable Now & Tomorrow Recommends

How can you take advantage of this new methodology in an organized manner? It's not that hard. Here's what we suggest:

- Set up a single e-mail address to be used exclusively for the receipt of invoices. Whoever is responsible for either processing the invoices that come into this address or forwarding them for approval should have the password, as should their backup and perhaps the department manager. The important thing is the e-mail account not belong to one person but several in case of absences etc.

- Set up a dedicated fax number to be used for accounts payable invoices only. Invoices can be retrieved throughout the day and integrated into the normal accounts payable workflow.

- Set up an e-fax facility to receive faxed invoices into an e-mail account. This should eliminate the problem of illegible invoices.

- Make sure your new e-mail address and fax number are included in all correspondence with vendors, especially your New Vendor Welcome kit.

- Convert as many vendor invoices as possible to this approach for delivering invoices. The benefits are overwhelming. Make sure you have management approval before starting the process,

The table below shows how several companies are making the most out of this new methodology. Paper invoices are fast becoming a thing of the past. Don't get left behind by ignoring the change—gear up for it. **DIYAP**

Best Practice Advice: How Four Companies Gain Efficiency Using E-mail/Fax to Receive Invoices

We started a new Shared Service Center in October 2006 to service all our divisions in North America. We have slowly brought on new divisions with the last one coming on board June 30, 2008. We have set up different company codes for each division to enable us to process invoices to the correct division. To aid us in processing, we have set up a different PO Box, e-mail address and fax number for vendors to send their invoices. This allows my staff to spend time processing the invoices instead of time sorting mail.

We accept faxed invoices. Set up a separate fax line for these invoices so they do not get lost in all the other items that come in via fax. Implement a fax server directly into your imaging system, and request invoices come to you via fax. It will save the time of scanning into your system.

When offered e-mail or faxed invoices, we requested e-mail for several reasons. We archive all of the invoices for a permanent record and also to have in case of lost invoices. All we have to do then is reprint and not bother having to call the company asking for a replacement. Since we share a fax machine with several other departments, faxes sometimes get lost or routed to a different department. Faxes also do not come through very clearly or they get cut off. Our main problem is trying to decipher the numbers. Is that a 6 or 3 or 8? This does not happen with an e-mail.

Our company formerly had a long-standing policy against accepting faxed invoices, which still stands. However, our management recently agreed to accept e-mailed invoices. E-mailed invoices are easily received, and have the added benefit of being forwarded to other departments if required for approval. The reason for the acceptance of e-mailed invoices is primarily due to the unreliability of the mail as well as many vendors getting our address wrong. Not receiving invoices due to address issues has caused many a payment delay and protracted argument over unpaid liabilities. **DIYAP**

AP Check Processes

- Exception Processing Diagnostic
- Check Request Forms Diagnostic
- Paper Check Safety Diagnostic
- Paper Check Elimination Checklist
- Un-cashed Checks
- Getting Vendors to Accept Electronic Payments
- Best Practice Advice: From Printing to Mailing: Do You Know Where Your Checks Are?
- Best Practice Advice: These Five Practices May be The Reason You Are Losing the Duplicate Payments War?
- Best Practice Advice: Practices to Avoid Check Request Fraud and Duplicate Payments
- Best Practice Advice: A Five-Step Plan to Get Rid of Rush Checks

The Exception Processing Diagnostic Quiz

Exception processing is where the costs and inefficiencies really add up in accounts payable—it's one of those silent, productivity sappers that rarely get attention. That's unfortunate because it really takes a chunk out of the bottom line. Frankly, not everyone realizes the full impact of overlooking this issue. While completely eliminating all exception processing is not really a realistic goal, acknowledging the problems it highlights and resolving them will lead to a more efficient, cost-effective accounts payable function.

Here's a list of just some of the problems that result from the exception processing issue:

- Extra time spent trying to resolve discrepancies;
- Lost early payment discounts;
- Time spent answering "where's my money" calls from vendors;
- Time spent processing second invoices sent when the first wasn't paid;
- Duplicate payments made when a few of those second invoices get paid;
- Time spent chasing invoices identified on statements as never received;
- Frayed vendor relationships;
- Disruptive relationship with purchasing;
- Increased number of rush checks; and, at public companies
- More items to be addressed during a S-Ox audit.

These are issues no organization wants to have, or if nothing else they'd like them kept to a minimum. Use our diagnostic to pinpoint the bottlenecks in your processes that could be exacerbating the problem. Then review the explanation of the issues and a look at what every organization can do to alleviate them. You'll notice as you read the questions that some of the solutions become self-evident. How many are actually in use in your organization?

1) Does your organization consider exception processing a problem that needs to be addressed? ___ Yes ___ No

2) Do you track disputed invoices? ___ Yes ___ No

3) If you do track disputed invoices by vendor, purchasing professional, and cause, do you regularly review your figures, identify the culprit, and take remedial action? ___ Yes ___ No

4) If you find a problem and try to fix it without success, do you raise the problem to the next level, i.e. take it to the person's supervisor? ___ Yes ___ No

5) Do you follow up on unresolved disputes at regular intervals? ___ Yes ___ No

6) Do you have a formal process for reviewing old invoices? ___ Yes ___ No

7) If your processors cannot get a dispute resolved within a reasonable amount of time (say 45 days) can they turn it over to a supervisor or manager for further handling? ___ Yes ___ No

8) Do you review statements both for credits and outstanding invoices? ___ Yes ___ No

9) If you identify outstanding invoices that have not reached your accounts payable department, do you try to track them down or get a copy? ___ Yes ___ No

10) Do you track the number, source, and reasons for rush checks? ___ Yes ___ No

11) If you do rush checks by vendor, purchasing professional, and cause, do you regularly review your figures, identify the culprit, and take remedial action? ___ Yes ___ No

12) If you find a rush check problem and try to fix it without success, do you raise the problem to the next level, i.e. take it to the person's supervisor? ___ Yes ___ No

13) Do you publish your check printing schedule along with the deadlines for inclusion in a check run? ___ Yes ___ No

14) Every time you issue a rush check, do you give the person requesting it a copy of your check printing cut-off schedule? ___ Yes ___ No

15) If you do track lost early payment discounts by vendor, purchasing professional, and cause, do you regularly review your figures, identify the culprit, and take remedial action? ___ Yes ___ No

16) If you find a lost early payment discount and try to fix it without success, do you raise the problem to the next level, i.e. take it to the person's supervisor? ___ Yes ___ No

17) Do you have a tolerances policy, i.e. allow processors to pay invoices within a small -dollar amount or percentage of the invoice? ____ Yes ____ No

18) Does your organization insist that all POs be filled out completely? ____ Yes ____ No

19) When your processors pay less than 100% of an invoice, do they include an explanation on the remittance advice? ____ Yes ____ No

20) Do you send a welcome letter to new vendors explaining your procedures for getting an invoice paid on time? ____ Yes ____ No

21) When you notice an invoice being sent to the wrong place, do you have a policy of notifying the vendor and having the invoice sent to the correct address or department? ____ Yes ____ No

22) Do you track disputed invoices by processor? ____ Yes ____ No

23) If you do track disputed invoices by processor, do you regularly review your figures to decide if the processor is the culprit and take remedial action? ____ Yes ____ No

24) Do you periodically have a third-party payment audit done, not only to recover duplicate and erroneous payments but to identify potential weaknesses in your process? ____ Yes ____ No

25) Do you periodically evaluate the accounts payable processes to see if AP may contribute to the exception processing problem? ____ Yes ____ No

See next page for discussion of the responses.

Explanation of the Best Practice Responses

1) Clearly, we believe the answer to this should be yes. Otherwise, we wouldn't have devoted so much space to the issue.

2) Similarly, we believe the first step in alleviating the problem is to track disputed invoices by vendor, purchasing professional, and cause for the dispute.

3) While tracking the disputed invoices by vendor and purchasing professional is the first step, doing something with the analysis after the fact should be your second step. If you don't identify the culprits and take remedial action you are wasting your time.

4) Occasionally after finding a problem and trying to fix it, you run into a brick wall because the culprit refuses to change. Escalate the issue, getting your supervisor involved if appropriate.

5) If you don't follow up on unresolved disputes at regular intervals, you'll end up with second invoices, duplicate payments, and aggravated vendors. Follow up quickly, while everyone still remembers the issues.

6) Every manager should have a formal process for reviewing their processors' old invoices. Sometimes just knowing the review is going to take place is enough to get the processor to address the problem.

7) Sometimes, despite your processors' best efforts, they can't get a dispute resolved within a reasonable amount of time (let's say 45 days). Again, it may be necessary to escalate the issue and turn it over to a supervisor or manager for further handling. If necessary, escalate again if the issue cannot be resolved.

8) Statements should be reviewed both for credits and outstanding invoices.

9) If the invoice is not in accounts payable but is on the statement, efforts should be made to find it. Otherwise, the odds are high that a rush check request will show up at some point.

10) Along the same lines as disputed invoices, tracking the number, source, and reasons for rush checks is another recommended best practice.

11) While tracking rush checks by vendor and purchasing professional is the first step, doing something with the analysis after the fact should be your second step. If you don't identify the culprits and take remedial action you are wasting your time.

12) Occasionally, after finding a problem and trying to fix it you run into a brick wall because the culprit refuses to change. Escalate the issue, getting your supervisor involved if appropriate.

13) This is simple and helps alleviate the rush check problem. There's really no reason the check printing schedule along with the deadlines for inclusion in a check run shouldn't be widely disseminated.

14) Another relatively easy-to-implement step to alleviate the rush check issue: give the person requesting it a copy of your check printing cut-off schedule to avoid future problems.

15) While tracking lost early payment discounts by vendor and purchasing professional is

the first step, doing something with the analysis after the fact should be your second step. If you don't identify the culprits and take remedial action you are wasting your time.

16) Occasionally, after finding a lost early payment discount problem and trying to fix it you run into a brick wall because the culprit refuses to change. Escalate the issue, getting your own supervisor involved if appropriate.

17) The issue of tolerances is a highly debatable one. Some organizations allow processors to pay invoices as long as the difference between the invoice and the purchase order is, let's say, less than $10 or less than one percent of the invoice amount. The processor is told to pay the lesser of the invoice or the PO. The proponents of this approach believe it is better not to waste time on small amounts of money. However those opposed say the small-dollar difference could actually mask two larger offsetting problems. The correct answer to this issue will depend on the nature of your business and your corporate culture. Whatever approach you decide on, make sure all your processors adhere to it or you could be opening a Pandora's box of troubles.

18) It is a recommended best practice for all organizations that all POs are filled out completely.

19) If your accounting system permits it, train your processors to include an explanation on the remittance advice when paying less than 100% of an invoice. This will eliminate many calls into accounts payable from vendors looking for an explanation of short paid invoices.

20) Start all relationships with new vendors on the right foot. Don't give them a chance to get it wrong. Send a welcome letter to new vendors explaining your procedures for getting an invoice paid on time.

21) When you notice an invoice being sent to the wrong place, immediately notify the vendor of the correct address or department. This is crucial when it comes to earning those valuable early payment discounts.

22) Tracking disputed invoices by processor is a good idea. While processors with high numbers may simply have the more difficult suppliers, it is also possible that they are part of the problem or are simply not working their disputed invoices.

23) If you evaluate your results by processor and decide the problem may not be outside the accounts payable department, provide the extra training the processor needs to reduce the number of her/his disputed invoices.

24) Third-party payment audit are a recommended best practice. In fact, the federal government mandates them for all agencies. Not only will they recover duplicate and erroneous payments but should also identify potential weaknesses in your process. Before you hire a firm, make sure you are going to get this valuable management report. After all, you don't want to pay them to do the same work over and over again each year, if you don't have to.

25) As much as we hate to admit it, occasionally, the problem with disputed invoices lies in the processes used in accounts payable. Periodically evaluate your processes to see if AP is contributing to the exception processing problem. If nothing else, it will provide the peace of mind that you are not. What's more, should someone angrily inquire about your processes, you can proudly say they have been thoroughly vetted. **DDIYAP**

The Check Request Form Diagnostic

Many organizations use check request forms to handle those miscellaneous payment needs that don't fall into the normal scope of invoice handling. Often the requirements for a check request are not clearly defined. Typically they are used to handle one-time payments or ongoing required payments, sometimes referred to as recurring payments. Some companies even use them to rush a payment through when the original invoice is lost. Others use them when there is no invoice. Sometimes they are employed for one-time vendors. And, at other times— well, you get the picture.

Do you allow multiple payee payments on one payment request form? ____Yes ____ No

Potential Issue: Tracking for duplicate payment purposes, GL coding, and possible fraud becomes difficult, if not impossible.

Do you allow internal company payment requests to be submitted without a specific supplier invoice reference number? ____Yes ____ No

Potential Issue: Duplicate payment checking routines are likely not to work.

Do you allow your processors to use their own unique descriptions or abbreviations when coding these payments? _____Yes ____ No

Potential Issue: Matching becomes difficult, if not impossible.

Do you use the check or payment request date as the invoice number for these items if there is no invoice number related to the request?

____Yes ____ No

Potential Issue: Numerous payments to different vendors will show up any time you try to research an invoice number. Additionally, if the vendor bills you frequently, such as an overnight mail carrier, you could end up with several payments to the same vendor with the same invoice number.

If you do use the check date as the invoice number, a practice that is already setting you up for trouble, (oops, I'm giving the answers away), does your process refuse to accept slashes, periods, hyphens, or any other sort of mark that is not a numeric? ____Yes ____ No

Potential Issue: Online tracking becomes virtually impossible.

The Correct Answers

You probably realize that answering affirmatively to any of these issues indicates you could have a problem and your process should be tightened up.

Regular readers of Accounts Payable Now & Tomorrow know that they should try and limit the use of check request forms as they are fraught with opportunities for duplicate payments. While we realize it is probably not possible to get away from them completely, we do recommend that the number of check request forms used be held to an absolute minimum. Of course, we say the same about Rush checks – which are often made using check request forms. **DIYAP**

Paper Check Safety Diagnostic

Checks pass through many different hands during the check production cycle. There are many opportunities, if proper care isn't taken, for someone to flitch a check and use it for nefarious purposes. Use our Best Practice checklist to determine if your organization has any weak links.

1. Is your preprinted check stock kept in a secure location with limited access? ____ Yes ____ No
2. Does your check stock have at least three safety features? ____ Yes ____ No
3. Do you keep a log tracking check numbers against number of checks printed? ____ Yes ____ No
4. Is your check log reconciled each time checks are printed to ensure no blank checks are missing? ____ Yes ____ No
5. After checks are printed, are they kept under lock and key if no one is working on them? ____ Yes ____ No
6. Are printed checks (before mailing) stored in a secure location with limited access? ____ Yes ____ No
7. When checks that do not require manual review or signature are ready for mailing, do you wait until right before the mail is taken to the post office before taking the checks to the mail room? ____ Yes ____ No
8. When checks are collated and taken for signature are they always being worked on or locked away, never being left unattended on a desk? ____ Yes ____ No
9. Do signers always check the backup and verify the accuracy of the amount, the payee and the accounting codes before signing? ____ Yes ____ No
10. Are signed checks returned immediately to accounts payable? ____ Yes ____ No
11. Are signers expressly forbidden to take checks home with them in the evening for review and signature? ____ Yes ____ No
12. When signed checks are returned to accounts payable, are they kept in a secure location (with limited access) until the backup is removed and the checks are put in envelopes for mailing? ____ Yes ____ No
13. Are voided and damaged checks marked as Void, the signature block removed and entered into a log? ____ Yes ____ No
14. Are all voided checks kept for review by audit? ____ Yes ____ No

Summary of Results

Total Number Marked Yes ______

Total Number Marked No ______

Explanation of the Check Safety Checklist Best Practices

By now you have probably figured out that the correct answer to each question is Yes. The idea behind these practices is to not leave checks alone or in a location where many people have access. One example is the mailroom or a locked room where numerous people have the key. By giving crooks as little opportunity as possible to grab one or more of your checks you are making it just a little bit harder for someone to help themselves to your organization's assets. And, that's part of the game in fraud prevention: make it so difficult for crooks that they turn their attention elsewhere. **DIYAP**

Could You Get Rid of More Paper Checks?

Have you found alternative payment methods for as many vendors as you can? We're willing to bet most readers could eliminate more. The checklist on page 8 will help you identify those remaining "opportunities" where you can make additional improvements.

The checklist is on the following page.

The AP Now Paper Check Elimination Checklist

Please select the payment mechanism you use to pay each of the following types of invoices. If you are using two approaches, check both. Then turn to page x to find out if you are taking full advantage of alternate payment vehicles.

Invoice Type	P-card	ACH	Wire	Check
Subscription	____	____	____	____
Utilities	____	____	____	____
Interest on Loans	____	____	____	____
Loan repayments (lump sum)	____	____	____	____
Office supplies	____	____	____	____
Temporary workers	____	____	____	____
Overnight shipping	____	____	____	____
Credit card bills (p-card & T&E)	____	____	____	____
Employees for T&E reimbursement	____	____	____	____
Taxes				
State	____	____	____	____
Federal	____	____	____	____
Sales and Use Tax	____	____	____	____
Social Security	____	____	____	____
Consultants	____	____	____	____
Other independent contractors	____	____	____	____
Cell phone bills for employees	____	____	____	____
Insurance premiums	____	____	____	____
Vendors who bill electronically	____	____	____	____
Vendors who send paper invoices	____	____	____	____
Invoices with early payment discounts	____	____	____	____
Invoices with late fees	____	____	____	____

A Discussion of the Best Practice Choices

Invoice Type **P-card ACH Wire Check**

Subscription __x__ _____ _____ _____

Virtually every publication takes credit cards and there is no reason to pay any other way. If your firm doesn't have a p-card program, the next best bet is ACH.

Utilities __x__ __x__ _____ __x__

A few utilities are starting to take credit cards. Check to see if yours is one of them. This is a great option; especially if you are looking to increase spend on the card for purposes of increasing rebates. If the p-card option doesn't work, ACH is the next best choice, unless your utility is not set up to accept electronic payments (most are). If all else fails, you may still have to pay with a paper check.

Interest on Loans _____ __x__ _____ _____

Virtually every financial institution accepts electronic payments. Make your interest payments using ACH and be assured your payment gets there on time.

Loan repayments (lump sum) _____ __x__ _____ _____

Same as above.

Office supplies __x__ _____ _____ _____

All office supply houses take credit cards and there is no good reason to pay for supplies any other way.

Temporary workers __x__ __x__ _____ _____

Many temporary agencies take credit cards. If not, investigate paying them via ACH.

Overnight shipping __x__ _____ _____ _____

Virtually all the overnight shipping companies take credit cards. This is an easy way to get those small dollar invoices out off the table.

Credit card bills (p-card & T&E) _ ____ __x__ _____ _____

Virtually all credit card companies will accept payments electronically. If you are at all concerned about getting the payment there by the due date, use the ACH. Even without concerns about the due date, ACH is the way to go.

Employees for T&E reimbursement _____ __x__ _____ _____

While you can't mandate ACH for payroll in many states, you can do so for T&E reimbursements. Expect pushback from a few employees who prefer checks for personal reasons. But, don't give in. ACH is the most efficient way to handle reimbursements.

Taxes

State ____ __x__ ____ ____
Federal ____ __x__ ____ ____
Sales and Use Tax ____ __x__ ____ ____
Social Security ____ __x__ ____ ____

Virtually all taxes can be paid using the ACH. A few states make it exceedingly difficult to pay that way and you might want to stick with checks for the short term. But, eventually we expect all states will make it easy for companies to pay them using the ACH.

Consultants ____ __x__ ____ ____

Make it part of your standard terms and conditions that you will pay via the ACH. Most of your consultants will appreciate it.

Other independent contractors ____ __x__ ____ ____

Same as above

Cell phone bills for employees __x__ __x__ ____ __x__

A few cell phone companies are accepting credit cards. Just be careful to make sure there is not a surge charge for paying this way. The second alternative is to pay using the ACH. This works well as long as you can clearly show which bill is being paid. As a last resort, use a paper check.

Insurance premiums ____ __x__ ____ ____

Most insurance companies not only accept electronic payments, they encourage it.

Vendors who bill electronically ____ __x__ ____ ____

Vendors who send their invoices to you using either a third-party e-invoicing process or by e-mail are likely to be interested in being paid electronically. Approach them to see if you can switch them away from paper checks. Most will be responsive.

Vendors who send paper invoices ____ __x__ ____ __x__

Just because a vendor is still sending paper invoices, does not mean they won't be receptive to being paid electronically. Ask and you may be surprised at the response.

Invoices with early payment discounts
____ __x__ ____ ____

Early payment discounts are a rare and valuable commodity. Increasingly, vendors are insisting that to earn those discounts, payments be made by the discount date. This is not always easy to do and paying electronically is a huge help in this regard. Put vendors offering early payment discounts at the top of your list of vendors to be converted from paper checks.

Invoices with late fees ____ __x__ ____ ____

Some vendors are becoming increasingly aggressive charging late fees. Even if your company has a policy of not paying these onerous fees, the vendor may still slap them on and try to charge them. A few are even using open credits to cover late fees. The best approach with these vendors is to pay electronically so you have definitive proof that the payment was made on time. **DIYAP**

Un-Cashed Checks: A Gold Mine or Additional Work for Accounts Payable?

It would be nice if every check sent out was cashed by the recipient as soon as it was received. That would certainly make life easier in accounts payable. But, is that the best course of action for the organization. Take our Un-cashed Checks Best Practice Diagnostic below and then read the explanation of the responses to determine what's best for all organizations and where yours stands on this issue.

1. Do you regularly follow up on un-cashed checks? ____ Yes ____ No
2. Do you keep all documentation when you reverse or checks? ____ Yes ____ No
3. When you void checks, do you document the reason and keep the backup? ____ Yes ____ No
4. When a check is returned as undeliverable, do you try and track down the vendor? ____ Yes ____ No
5. Is the person who does your bank recs different than the person who handles your Unclaimed Property? ____ Yes ____ No
6. Do you put a stop payment on all lost or stolen checks before reissuing them? ____ Yes ____ No
7. Do you periodically update vendor contact information with the vendor? ____ Yes ____ No
8. Do you report un-cashed checks to the states as unclaimed property? ____ Yes ____ No
9. Do you write un-cashed checks off to miscellaneous income? ____ Yes ____ No
10. When a check is returned as undeliverable, do you do nothing? ____ Yes ____ No

	Column A	**Column B**
	Yes	No
Total 1-8	______	______
	No	Yes
Total 9-10	______	______
Grand Total	______	______

A Discussion of the Best Practice Responses

Hopefully you all have a 10 as the Grand Total for column A. If not, let's take a look at where you might have steered wrong.

1. Regularly following up on un-cashed checks is a good practice for several reasons. For starters it is required that you do certain due diligence before turning un-cashed checks over to the states as unclaimed property. The sooner you take this step, the more like-

ly you are to find the rightful owner. Most organizations do this when a check has been outstanding for 60 or 90 days. A few do it at 45 days.

2. There are many reasons why you might need to reverse a check. It can be as simple as the check got damaged in printing and you need to reissue it. Or, it could be issued on the wrong account or you could discover the payment had already been made. All of these are legitimate business reasons. Both your internal auditors and the state unclaimed property auditors are likely to question why the reversal was made. Keeping all documentation that backs why you reversed the check is a recommended best practice so you are not overridden when you can't prove your reason. And, without this documentation your reversed check may be viewed as unclaimed property by an aggressive state auditor.

3. Voided checks present a unique challenge. Like reversed checks discussed above, they usually are voided for legitimate business reasons. And like reversed checks, keeping the documentation as to the reason for the void is crucial for the same reasons.

4. When a check is returned as undeliverable, tracking down the payee is a good idea. You will have to do due diligence on un-cashed checks before turning them over to the state so why not get started the moment the check is returned. If you can track them down at that point, you'll avoid more tedious work in the future.

5. Segregation of duties is not something one automatically thinks about when it comes to un-cashed checks. But, like everything else in accounts payable, it is related. The person who does your bank recs should be someone other than the person who handles your Unclaimed Property. Why? Because in more than one instance, a person knowing about an un-cashed check has changed the name on the company records so the funds are turned over to the state not in the name of the legitimate owner but in another name so the employee can collect the money. Now, if you are thinking the company isn't harmed financially by this chicanery, you would be wrong. When the rightful owner shows up to claim the funds, the company would have to make the payment and would not be able to get it back from the state as it would not realize what had happened. This unfortunately has happened to more than one organization where the fraud was uncovered before the funds were reported. How many times it went on undetected is, of course, unknown.

6. Putting a stop payment on all lost or stolen checks before reissuing them is just good business sense. In a small number of cases, the original check will eventually show up and be cashed. In many cases, this would be done not in an attempt to defraud your organization but simply because no one realized it was a duplicate payment. If for example, the payment was sent to a bank lockbox no one would realize a check had been reissued.

7. Periodically update vendor contact information with the vendor is critical if you want to be able to easily contact the vendor in cases of fraud or un-cashed checks. If the information isn't updated regularly, you are unlikely to be able to get a current employee on the phone.

8. As you've probably deduced by this time, un-cashed checks should be reported to the states as unclaimed property. There are a few states that have weak B2B exemptions, but in order for the exemption to hold up, there have to be several convoluted scenarios. Rather than rely on the B2B exemption, employ best practices as discussed above to eliminate reportable un-cashed checks.

9. Writing un-cashed checks off to miscellaneous income is a really bad practice and one

that is almost guaranteed to bring trouble when unclaimed property auditors show up. It was an old practice – that was never right – but one that worked more than occasionally in the past. Now, one of the first thing unclaimed property auditors ask for when they show up is your miscellaneous income account. Expect to remit everything in that account attributable to un-cashed checks to the state. So, as a best practice, never write off un-cashed checks as miscellaneous income. Figure out where they belong and account for them correctly!

10. When a check is returned as undeliverable, doing nothing is not an acceptable practice. Eventually, you will have to do something to get those items off your books and bank recs. Start as soon as the check is returned and you'll have a much better chance of resolving the issue.

So in response to the question on page one, do un-cashed checks represent a gold mine or additional work for accounts payable, we're afraid the answer lies squarely in the additional work column. Those who view them as a gold mine are in for a rude awakening when they undergo an unclaimed property audit. **DIYAP**

Getting Your Vendors to Accept e-Payments

You've finally convinced a supplier to bill you electronically. Now, you're faced with the challenge of convincing them to accept payment electronically and it's not going well. Have you done everything you can? Use our Best Practice checklist below to make sure you've hit all their issues.

1. Have you walked the proverbial mile in their shoes, figuring out what their issues for not taking electronic payments? ____ Yes ____ No

2. Have you addressed the issue of ensuring your supplier gets the remittance advice information needed to apply cash? ____ Yes ____ No

3. Have you offered to e-mail remittance information to more than one person in your suppliers' organization, if that would help? ____ Yes ____ No

4. If you've tried to re-negotiate payment terms in an attempt to share the mail float, have you considered moving forward on the same payment terms, if the supplier refuses to budge on this issue? ____ Yes ____ No

5. Have you pointed out the cost savings of not having to either take checks to the bank or pay the charges associated with a bank lockbox? ____ Yes ____ No

6. Have you pointed out that electronic payments never get 'lost in the mail'? ____ Yes ____ No

7. If a rush payment is required, do you insist on making it electronically so the vendor can experience the benefits of electronic payments first hand? ____ Yes ____ No

8. If the vendor is reluctant to provide its bank account information, have you explained to them the controls you have in place to safeguard their banking information? ____ Yes ____ No

9. If the vendor is reluctant to provide its bank account information, have you offered

them the option of using an intermediary, such as UPIC? ___ Yes ___ No

10. Have you revisited the issue of accepting electronic payments with vendors who initially turned you down? ___ Yes ___ No

A Discussion of the Best Practice Responses

Clearly the ideal response to all items on the checklist on the prior page is yes. While most think of a few of the issues, some are not addressed. Let's take a look at how each of these issues, if handled correctly, is likely to improve your chances of getting vendors to accept electronic payments.

1. By putting yourself in the vendor's shoes, you should be able to figure out what their issues are for not wanting to take electronic payments. Once you've identified the problem, you can then devise a solution that will make both sides happy.

2. Perhaps the most common reasons vendor are reluctant to receive payments electronically has to do with their inability to coordinate the remittance advice information needed to apply cash. If they can't get that into the right hands, the cash application task becomes a nightmare for them.

3. Recognizing that remittance information is critical, offering to e-mail remittance information to more than one person in your suppliers' organization sometimes helps. If you can automate the process, whether you e-mail their information to one person or 50 should not be difficult or expense.

4. If you've tried to re-negotiate payment terms in an attempt to share the mail float, and the vendor refuses, don't give up. Consider that you still benefit even if you don't get any change in payment terms. True your cash flow will be affected, but the other benefits far outweigh that minor drawback. So, whether it's fair or not, look at the big picture and how electronic payments benefit your company. Consider moving forward with those vendors who refuse to budge when it comes to renegotiating payment terms.

5. When evaluating the concept of electronic payments, some vendors forget that there are cost savings associated with not having to either take checks to the bank or pay the charges associated with a bank lockbox. While these are not huge, they do add up. Make sure your vendor understands the full financial impact.

6. If you have vendors who always seem to lose your checks, you might point out that electronic payments never get 'lost in the mail' or on someone's desk. There is a 100% audit trail and everyone can see exactly when the payment was made as well as when it was received.

7. While it is difficult to force vendors to accept electronic payments if they don't wish to be paid in that manner, there is one exception. Most will take electronic payments if the initial payment is late and they have made a collection call. This is especially true at the end of a quarter for those collectors who get bonuses based on collection results. If your company policy is that all rush payments are to be made electronically, the vendor will probably agree. Once that happens and the vendor experiences the benefits of electronic payments many are happy to continue being paid this way. This is certainly an example of making lemonade from lemons.

8. A few vendors are reluctant to provide bank account information out of security concerns. If you explain to them the controls you have in place to safeguard their banking

information they just may change their minds. This is one time when having a vendor self-service portal, where the vendor enters its own bank account information, will help.

9. Sometimes, even after you've explained how you safeguard information, the vendor is still reluctant to provide its bank account information. In this case you might offer them the option of using an intermediary, such as UPIC. Information about this service can be found at upic.com

10. When it comes to electronic payments, many companies do eventually change their minds. Some have been forced to accept payments by another vendor and others have just seen the light or adjusted their processes to accommodate electronic payments. Others may have had a change in management. No only means not right now, it doesn't necessarily mean no forever. Periodically, revisit the issue of accepting electronic payments with vendors who initially turned you down. You might be surprised to see which ones have changed their policy with regards to accepting electronic payments.

There is one last approach you can try, although few are willing to go this step. A few vendors are now insisting, as part of their contracts and/or terms and conditions, that the vendor accepts payment electronically. They are refusing to issue paper checks. Before going this route, you want to make sure that management is in agreement with this stance and that purchasing is on board. Representatives from the purchasing group will have to include this issue in discussions with new vendors as part of their initial conversations. And of course, existing vendors will have to be contacted and converted. **DIYAP**

Best Practice Advice: From Printing to Mailing: Do You Know Where Your Checks Are?

Remember the old commercial that asked, "It's 10:00 p.m.; do you know where your children are?" Well, think about your paper checks. Do you know where they are between the time they are printed and when they go to the post office for mailing? If you're not careful, all your strong internal controls will be for naught if someone walks off with a few of your checks. Let's look at some of the vulnerable points.

After Printing and Before Signing

Do you collate checks with backup before taking them to be signed? Most organizations do. Depending on the number of checks and your signing requirements, this can be a huge job. I know one organization that can spend two days a week on this odious task. Here are some issues to consider about this part of the process:

1) Where are the checks kept after printing but before collating?
2) Where is the collating done? Out in the open where both employees and visitors frequently walk by or in a secure location?
3) If the collating is not finished by the end of the day, where are the checks stored?
4) Who does the collating?
5) Where are the checks kept between collating and bringing them to an authorized signer?

When the Checks Are Out for Signing?

How often do you walk down the hall and glance into an authorized signer's empty office only to see checks lying on his or her desk? The truth is this is a familiar sight at virtually every organization that has manually signed checks—and it's a risk. Whether a disgruntled employee, or one with personal financial issues, or an outsider with larceny in his or her heart walks by, these checks are an invitation to potential trouble.

Similarly, when the signer completes signing, do they immediately return the checks or call for someone to pick them up? And, if they call for someone, do they stay with the signed checks or just leave them waiting? Should checks be stolen at this stage of the operation, they would probably clear your bank since the positive pay file is, in all likelihood, already transmitted. Should the bank ever discover your lax practices you could be deemed not exercising reasonable care—and therefore liable for the loss.

When the Checks Are Signed and Returned

Once the checks are returned, in most organizations, the backup must be removed and the checks put into an envelope for mailing. Is this done immediately or do the folders with the signed checks lie around for a few hours or days? If the stuffing of the envelopes isn't completed by the close of business, where are those signed checks stored?

This is one of the most critical control points. In most organizations, the positive pay file has been transmitted and the checks are signed and viable. A crook doesn't have to do much to get the check cashed. It is recommended that these checks be stored under lock and key if they are not mailed immediately.

To be perfectly honest, it's a good idea to keep all checks locked away if they are not being worked on—but it is critical if the check has been signed.

And finally, once the checks have been stuffed into their envelopes, are they taken to the mailroom? It is highly recommended that they *not* be taken to the mailroom until right before the mail goes to the post office. The reason is simple. In many organizations the mailroom has numerous outsiders coming in and out, making deliveries, picking up packages, etc. You have no idea who those people are. And if they happen to have a penchant for check fraud, they will recognize what's in those envelopes you have so nicely lined up for mailing.

As those reading this are ever so painfully aware, you cannot completely stop check fraud. But you can make it more difficult for those looking to perpetrate it on your organization. By appropriately addressing the issue of where your checks are at every step of the cycle, you will have made it all the harder for them. And, hopefully, they will turn their eyes to another target. **DIYAP**

Best Practice Advice: Losing the Duplicate Payments War? These Five Practices May Be to Blame!

1. Invoices paid by check request forms in case of emergency can inadvertently create a situation where the duplicate payment can slip through. Since the three-way match is often not utilized when processing check requests, the purchase order and receiver often remain open. Then when the original invoice finally shows up in accounts payable for payment it is processed through the standard payment process and paid a second time. What's even worse is these check request payments are sometimes made without backup so tying them to a particular invoice is difficult if not impossible.

2. The data entry practice for entering invoice numbers occasionally fosters duplicate payments. Most organizations know they should incorporate invoice coding standards and have done so. This greatly decreases the chance of a duplicate payment. However, what some don't crack down on are the nifty ways processors sometimes have for working around the controls. Most processors know that by adding a space or a period or another digit or letter to an invoice number they can force the invoice through their system.

3. Payments made outside AP by employees not fully schooled in strict accounts payable routines can cause duplicates. With the move to ACH and p-cards, a decent number of organizations are allowing payments to be made by employees outside the accounts payable organization. On the face of it, there is nothing wrong with this. However, if these employees are not trained using the strict coding standards employed in accounts payable, or they do not correctly close out the purchase order and/or the receiving document, the chance for a duplicate payment looms. Additionally, although not related to payments, not properly closing these related documents could lead to inaccurate financial statements and additional work as someone has to review open receivers.

4. Lack of a single payment mechanism to pay each vendor often results in payment being made by both p-card and invoice. While it is a theoretical best practice that each vendor be paid using only one payment vehicle, that practice is not always feasible. A few vendors claim they cannot suppress the printing of the invoice and in theory most are marked either with a zero balance due or that the invoice has been paid by p-card.

5. Not sorting out duplicate copies of invoices. In the past it was relatively easy to discern a faxed copy of an invoice or a second invoice. Today, with the advances in printing and e-mail, it is no longer so simple and it's often impossible to tell which is the original and which is the copy. Suppliers regularly send pdfs of invoices— and who can spot if it's the first time the invoice was received or a later copy? While it's still a good idea to refuse to pay from copies or faxes, that approach won't provide you with the same protection it did just a few short years ago. **DIYAP**

Best Practice Advice: Practices to Avoid Check Request Fraud and Duplicate Payments

Ahhh...check requests, that ubiquitous form used to request payments for all sorts of things. Theoretically a solution (by making it easy to request a payment when an invoice is missing) in reality it can create numerous headaches for accounts payable, not to mention causing duplicate payments by the boatload. Here's a look at some of the problems surrounding check requests and a few suggestions on avoiding them.

Background

Check requests are used in most organizations to request payment when an invoice is not available or was never provided. Ideally, there should be backup documentation augmenting the check request and providing details regarding the payment amount, the payee, and the reason for the payment. Since most payments made on check request forms will *not* go through the rigorous three-way match in accounts payable, the documentation supporting the check request is of utmost importance.

The one exception to this is those organizations that require a check request for every single payment. This is not a best practice, although some organizations with unique industry or regulatory requirements might find it necessary to go this route.

Where Check Requests Cause Problems

Check requests forms are often used to accommodate rush check requests. These are one-time payments made to vendors outside the normal invoice submission process. Typically this happens when a payment is late and the upset vendor threatens to put the organization on credit hold.

Whether the check request form is used for a rush check or simply because the invoice has been misplaced if the proper documentation is not attached the chances for a duplicate payment skyrocket. Ideally the attached documentation should be the original invoice. Of course, if it were available, there might be no need for the check request form.

Without the invoice to perform the three-way match, the purchase order and receiver often remain open on the organization's books. This can blossom into two types of problems. The most obvious is a duplicate payment made when the invoice finally shows up and is paid in accounts payable.

The less obvious issue is what happens to the open receivers and purchase orders when the financial statements are prepared. And, as discussed in prior issues of *Accounts Payable Now & Tomorrow*, there is a chance that the states could view open receivers as unclaimed property.

The final problem relates to fraud. Alas, a great number of fraudulent payments, more than we'd like to think, are issued on check requests. How is this possible? The most obvious answer is a crooked employee fills out the check request form and either convinces an authorized signer to sign it or forges the signature himself.

The other way that fraud occurs with a check request form is in response to an irate vendor claiming non-payment. Some vendors have learned if they get on the phone and are generally abusive with the accounts payable staff threatening credit holds, they can sometimes get a harried controller to sign off on a check request form authorizing the payment. In one of the most egregious examples of this type of fraud a vendor pulled this screaming stunt every month for 18 months—getting double payment for each one. With murky documentation attached to each form, it was difficult to find the duplicates until the entire vendor file was pulled and reviewed.

Best Check Request Practices

There are a number of steps any organization to make the check request form work as it is intended without introducing the problems discussed above. Begin by requiring documentation for every check request form. If an invoice, or copy of an invoice, is not available, attach a copy of the contract, an e-mail detailing requirements, or whatever is available. Great care should be taken to avoid sending in the form without any supporting documents

In the extreme cases where no documentation is available—and you know that will happen at some point—require an extra signature of a very high-level executive within the organization, perhaps the controller or the CFO. The person making the request should be ready with a *really* good explanation for why the check should be issued without documentation. Requests without documentation should be few and far between. If there are outstanding POs and receivers related to these requests, that information should be included on the form so accounts payable can extinguish them when the payment is made.

If by some miracle, there is an invoice attached to the check request form, perform the normal three-way match extinguishing both the purchase order and the open receiver.

Reducing the Number of Check Request Forms

If you only have a few check request forms each month to process, there is, in all likelihood, little you can do to decrease the number of them. Like rush checks, a small number is inevitable

If you get more than a few, for several months, track the requests keeping a log noting:

- The requestor;
- The payee;
- The date of the request; and
- The reason for the request.

When you have the data for a few months, take it out and analyze it. Are most of your requests coming from a few requestors? In that case you might want to have some discussions with those involved to determine where the problem lies.

But before you do that, take a look at the vendors receiving the payments. Are a suspiciously high number of these requests going to the same vendor? This could mean one of two things. The less sinister explanation is that there is a problem somewhere in the process that needs to be fixed so the vendor can receive payment through the normal cycle. The more ominous reason is that there is an ongoing fraud.

If you suspect fraud, do not approach the individuals involved. Get all your facts lined up ask your immediate supervisor to review them and if you both agree something is fishy, get HR involved. They will know the correct way to approach this situation. Discretion is crucial in these cases for two reasons. First, you could be wrong and, secondly, if you are correct, you don't want to tip your hand before the experts decide how to approach the matter.

Check request forms are a necessary evil. Work hard to implement best practices surrounding them and the troubles they cause will be held to a minimum. **DIYAP**

Best Practice Advice: A Five-Step Plan to Get Rid of Rush Checks

Do you have documented policies and procedures to handle rush checks? Did you know this could be the first sign of a well-run organization with problems in their accounts payable process? If this has you scratching your head, let me explain. Rush checks are one of the leading causes of both duplicate payments and fraud. Plus, they can also get you into trouble on a Sarbanes-Oxley audit if you have too many of them. While everyone understands that no business runs so smoothly that the occasional rush check won't be called for, more than a few each month is a sign that the payment function is just not running as well as it should.

Why The Fuss?

If fraud and duplicate payments aren't enough to convince you that your organization shouldn't permit rush checks (also sometimes called ASAP checks or manual checks), here are a few more reasons to get rid of them.

1) Rush checks are very expensive to issue when you take into account the time it takes to produce them.
2) Issuing rush checks disrupts the accounts payable function making it less efficient.
3) More than a few rush checks demonstrate poor internal controls.
4) When rush checks are permitted on a regular basis, the rest of the company gets lazy and makes no attempt to avoid them.
5) Rush checks often are sent by overnight delivery making them even more expensive.

The Action Plan

If you want to put a serious dent in the number of rush checks issued in your organization, try the following:

- Convince management that they really are a bad idea. Use the facts discussed in this article along with some numbers demonstrating just how expensive a rush check actually is.
- Make it *really* difficult for someone to get a rush check. This could include requiring a sign-off from the CFO along with an explanation of why this payment could not wait for the regular check cycle. If the CFO is a believer in eliminating rush checks, this step alone may do the trick.
- Identify the causes for rush checks by keeping a log of who requests them and why. After you have a few weeks or months activity, you should be able to identify trends and culprits (both at your company and on the outside) and then fix the problem.
- Identify duplicate payments made with a rush or manual check. Bring this to the attention of everyone involved and management. There's nothing like seeing a large-dollar amount associated with rush checks to put an end to the practice.

Insist on paying electronically instead of by check. When you do get a request for a rush check, insist on ACH payment. Hopefully you will convince the recipient to be paid electronically in the future eliminating them from future rush check pools.

By relentlessly keeping after the issue and refusing to let it grow you can make some serious headway in reducing the number of those time-wasting, productivity-sucking, rush check requests. **DIYAP**

AP Interdepartmental Processes

- Identifying Problems in the Purchase-to-Pay Process Diagnostic
- Master Vendor File Diagnostic
- Does Your Accounts Payable Department Play Well with Others? Diagnostic
- Best Practice Advice: Master Vendor File Best Practices
- Best Practice Advice: 8 Simple Tactics to Reduce Stress in the AP/Purchasing Relationship

Identifying Problems in the Purchase-to-Pay Process Diagnostic

Problems in the purchase-to-pay process manifest themselves when the invoice gets to accounts payable. The process is strewn with opportunities for companies to lose money through inefficient, if not downright shoddy, practices. For the most part, the professionals who run the accounts payable operation know these practices should be overhauled but often don't have the political clout to insist on the change. Sarbanes-Oxley has changed some of that but there is still room for improvement at many organizations. Let's look at some of the problems that occur in accounts payable when the purchase-to-pay process.

1)Do you fail to earn (and take) more than 10% of the early payment discounts your firm is entitled to? ____Yes ____ No

Potential Issue: The primary issue is the loss of the early payment discount, which in the current low-interest-rate environment may represent the best investment opportunity your company has. Secondarily, failure to earn early payment discounts can be symptomatic of bigger operational issues.

2) Does your accounts payable staff often pay invoices that are marked "Copy, Duplicate, or Second request"? ____Yes ____ No

Potential Issue: Paying from copies is one of the biggest causes of duplicate payments. Best-practice accounts payable departments make it a policy never to pay from copies unless extenuating circumstances are proved.

3) Do you issue more than five manual (rush or ASAP) checks each month? ____Yes ____ No

Potential Issue: Rush checks indicate a breakdown in sound invoice processing procedures. While every firm has an occasional slip up or need when a check must be issued outside the normal check production cycle, more than a few indicates a serious problem. If paying from copies is the number one cause for duplicate payments, paying with rush checks outside the normal cycle is the second most common cause.

4) Does your staff spend tons of time tracking down delinquent payments for vendors looking to be paid? ____Yes ____ No

Potential Issue: Inefficient processes lead to tons of time wasted in the accounts payable department.

5) Has your company ever been put on credit hold by a key supplier because an invoice had not been paid (not because of financial difficulties)? ____Yes ____ No

Potential Issue: Yikes—this one is really bad. While key suppliers can sometimes behave like pampered princesses, to get one to the point that it puts you on credit hold because of non-payment signals an almost complete breakdown in effective processing procedures. The problem is just as likely to be outside of the accounts payable department as it is within the group. However, that will not matter when production starts screaming.

6) Do you purge your master vendor file at least once a year? ____Yes ____ No

Potential Issue: Inactive vendors in the master vendor file are an open invitation to employee fraud. Additionally, it makes it easier for duplicate payments to slip through.

Explanation of the Purchase-to-Pay Process Diagnostic

Once again, all the questions have the same answers. (And, yes, we are going to devise quizzes in the future where an answer key will be required.) Even one response of yes is not really acceptable as these are all serious issues. Not only do inefficient processes cost in terms of wasted time when it comes to payments, they often—as was demonstrated above—open the door for fraudsters and duplicate or erroneous payments.

Most of the problems discussed were symptomatic of bigger problems. To diagnose the source of your problems try the following:

1) Begin by flow charting the process as it should work including estimated time frames for each step in the transaction.

2) Then flow chart the process as it actually works including your estimates of the time actually spent on each task. Include in that second chart estimates for time spent on the various additional steps. This might include the issuing of rush checks, time spent on calls from vendors either looking for their money or with an inquiry about a partial payment, etc.

3) Compare the two charts.

From your comparison you should be able to pinpoint two items.

1) By looking at those areas where the actual time spent was much longer than the ideal time you can identify those areas that need further investigation. Clearly something is going wrong and the process at that point needs to be reengineered or procedures need to be enforced.

2) Using the information gathered above estimate how much extra time is being spent on the payment process. Convert this into a dollar figure using the average salaries of the employees performing the tasks. Don't forget to include the cost for the time spent on extra tasks that the poor processes generate. Add to that any lost income (of lost dis-

counts etc.).

As noted above, the source of the problem is often outside of accounts payable. This can make fixing the issue tricky especially if the root cause is a department or individual who is at odds with accounts payable. Depending on where the breakdown is you made need support from management in both your department and elsewhere.

Often the professionals handling payments know where the problem is, they don't need to do the diagnostic suggested above. But there is a very good reason for doing it. The analysis will arm you with the data you need to enforce the procedural changes needed to improve your payment processes. It will provide you with the metrics and ammunition to, at the very least, force a discussion, if not the actual change itself. **DIYAP**

Master Vendor File Diagnostic

Often overlooked in the scramble to get invoices processed in a timely manner, good master vendor file policies are critical to eliminating duplicate payments and deterring fraud. To be blunt, this is a topic that does not get the attention it deserves in some organizations. What's worse, the occasional disgruntled employee recognizes these weaknesses and if so inclined also knows how to take advantage of these flaws. Use AP Now's Master Vendor File Best Practice Checklist to determine if your practices strong enough to prevent the problems already mentioned.

The Master Vendor File Best Practice Checklist

Part One:

1) Do you cleanse your master vendor file periodically, ideally at least once a year? ___ Yes ___ No
2) Is the data on inactive vendors saved? ___ Yes ___ No
3) Do you have a strict vendor naming convention for setting up vendors in the master vendor file? ___ Yes ___ No
4) Does your master vendor file naming convention match the coding standard for entering invoice data? ___ Yes ___ No
5) Do you have a form that must be completed before a new vendor is added to the master vendor file? ___ Yes ___ No
6) Do you require a second level of approval before a new vendor is added to the master vendor file? ___ Yes ___ No
7) Do you regularly (ideally weekly) run a report detailing all changes, additions and deletions to the master vendor file? ___ Yes ___ No
8) Is your report showing changes to the master vendor file reviewed closely by a senior level executive? ___ Yes ___ No

Part Two:

1) Can employees who notice a vendor missing from the master vendor file simply add the vendor? ___ Yes ___ No
2) Can employees who create purchase orders make changes to the master vendor file? ___ Yes ___ No
3) Can employees who process invoices make changes to the master vendor file? ___ Yes ___ No
4) Can employees who approve invoices for payment make changes to the master vendor file? ___ Yes ___ No
5) Can employees who handle checks (in any capacity) make changes to the master vendor file? ___ Yes ___ No

Explanation of the Master Vendor File Checklist Best Practices

By now you probably realize that you would have responded Yes to all the questions in Part One and No to those in part two if your master vendor file procedures employ best practices.

If any of your responses did not match the suggested practices, review your operations to figure out how you can change them to accommodate the recommended procedures. We realize this may mean moving the responsibility for the master vendor file out of accounts payable and/or purchasing to another part of the accounting department. **DIYAP**

User Friendly Accounts Payable Department Best Practice Checklist

Do your vendors and employees outside accounts payable cringe when they have to have any interaction with the accounts payable staff? Does your accounts payable department have the reputation of being the 'black hole'? Or perhaps, your department operates pretty well but there is the occasional flare up with outsiders that ends up with the manager being called in to "explain." None of these situations are good and there are ways you can improve. Take our Is Your AP Department User Friendly? Quiz on page x to identify ways you can improve your relations with outsiders as well as the efficiency of your accounts payable function.

1) Does the accounts payable department respond to all inquiries within 24 hours? ___ Yes _____ No

2) If you have not resolved an issue within 24 hours, do you still call or email to update the person who made the original inquiry giving them an estimated date for resolution of their issue? ___ Yes _____ No

3) Do you publish you check production cutoff schedule so everyone knows exactly when an invoice must be received approved in accounts payable in order to be included in the next check run? ___ Yes _____ No

4) Do you track and measure your inquiry response time? ___ Yes _____ No

5) Do you track disputed invoices to make sure all are resolved within a reasonable amount of time? ___ Yes _____ No

6) Do you follow up with processors and/or purchasing staff who do not resolve disputes in a timely manner? ___ Yes _____ No

7) Do you track the cause or reason for each disputed invoice? ___ Yes _____ No

8) Do you track the processor associated with each disputed invoice? ___ Yes _____ No

9) Do you track the vendor associated with each disputed invoice? ___ Yes _____ No

10) Do you track the purchaser associated with each disputed invoice? ___ Yes _____ No

11) Do you periodically analyze the causes, processor, vendors and purchasers involved with disputed invoices to identify problems in your process? ___ Yes _____ No

12) Any time your accounts payable policies and or procedures are updated, are they shared with everyone in the organization? ___ Yes _____ No

13) Do you send a welcome letter to new vendors letting them know what they need to do to get paid on time? ___ Yes _____ No

14) Are you honest with vendors, telling them exactly when they will be paid instead of just telling them what they want to hear to get them off the phone? ___ Yes _____ No

15) Has your staff ever received any customer service or working with other departments training? ___ Yes _____ No

16) If you have only one or two people handling inquiries, have you assigned the task to the staffers with the best people skills? ___ Yes _____ No

17) Do you send email reminders to those who need to get information to accounts payable before key dates, like the year-end close? ___ Yes _____ No

18) When you have to give unpleasant news to a vendor, do you alert the purchasing professional responsible for the accounts? ___ Yes _____ No

19) Is your Travel & Entertainment (T&E) policy detailed enough so employees won't misinterpret what's covered and more importantly, what's not? ___ Yes _____ No

20) Are you aware of which executives are laggards when it comes to approving employee expense reimbursement? Are you a little more lenient with those employees if they miss a cutoff date and have a credit card bill due? ____ Yes _____ No

21) Do you treat everyone equally, not doing special favors for friends, while demanding all other employees comply strictly with T&E guidelines and cutoff schedules? ____ Yes _____ No

22) Do you review and update both your accounts payable policy and procedures manual and your T&E policy at least once a year? ____ Yes _____ No

23) Should one of your processors find payment terms on an invoice that are more favorable than the ones currently being offered to your FIRM, do you alert purchasing so they can use that intelligence when negotiating the next contract? ____ Yes _____ No

24) Do you offer to run aggregate accounts payable data so purchasing can use it to negotiate preferred supplier contracts? ____ Yes _____ No

25) Do you have an accounts payable newsletter for your company, updating employees on changes in cutoff schedules, changes in policy, introducing new staff and addressing common errors? ____ Yes _____ No

Total ____ Yes _____ No

Clearly the best practice answer to all these questions is a resounding Yes. Please see page xx for a discussion of why each of these policies makes good business sense.

A Discussion of Best Practices that Will Make The AP Function More User Friendly

Basically, accounts payable is a service organization. It processes invoices and makes payments on behalf of its "customers," verifies employee expense reports and reimburses where appropriate and conducts business so the organization is regulatory compliant. Viewing the function as a service provider means customer service is an issue and an important one. Many accounts payable departments take the attitude that they are the customer and "the customer is always right." This approach is what earns those departments a black eye and earns them the reputation of being "difficult."

The purpose of this checklist is to identify those behaviors that are either missing or are not properly administered and correct them. The items included are those that, if implemented correctly, will make interacting with accounts payable more pleasant and earn the department a reputation for being "user friendly." All this can be done without sacrificing efficiency.

Changing the way the department is viewed is a long-term project. However, it is something virtually everyone can do. The following principles will drive the process:

- Eliminate as many of the problems as you can before they occur.
- Provide clear and detailed information to both vendors and other employees so there are as few misunderstandings as possible.
- Address problems quickly and fix underlying processes, where required, when a new issue emerges.

Now, let's take a look at the nitty-gritty details to determine where you might want to make some process improvements and why.

and 2. By quickly responding to inquiries you not only improve the relationship with the person who called, you reduce the number of calls coming into accounts payable as the person won't be calling back to follow up in less than a stellar mood.

3. By providing check run information in advance you eliminate the confrontations with folks who have just missed the cutoff. This is especially important in those organizations with weekly or bi-weekly check runs.

4. through 11. By tracking every possible detail related to disputed invoices it may be possible to identify root problems creating the discrepant invoice. With this information you can then work with the parties responsible to change the process to eliminate the problem. Without this detailed information it is difficult to find the glitch and to convince the transgressors to change their ways.

12. and 13. As in #3, educating your customers about your policies is the best way to keep everyone on the same page – and happy.

14. Telling a vendor that he won't be paid for two weeks might not make that supplier happy. But in the long run, his annoyance with your organization will be a lot less than if you tell him "the check's in the mail" when it is not. Those follow up calls when the promised payment is not received can get downright ugly.

15. and 16. Staff training is always a good idea, no matter what the topic. Dealing with third parties is rarely addressed. While a few people are instinctively good when it comes to dealing with customers, the rest of us need a few pointers.

17. Unfortunately, accounts payable requirements are frequently the last thing on the mind of busy executives. If you only reimburse T&E once a month, avoid those ugly scenes and send out a reminder email. Similarly, send reminders around important dates such as the dates yearend information is needed.

18. By alerting purchasing that a vendor is unhappy you can accomplish two goals. First, they will know to expect an unhappy supplier call but more importantly, you can give them the facts. Then, if a vendor calls and distorts the story, the purchasing professional is armed and ready.

19. There are more T&E disputes over what's not explicitly spelled out in the policy than over anything else. And those disagreements can be quite dreadful. Avoid those nobody-told-me-we-weren't-supposed-to arguments by documenting requirements in the T&E policy.

20. Those organizations that require employees to use their own credit cards and then file for reimbursement have an added stress point in accounts payable. Most employees need their reimbursement check in order to pay the credit card bill. When a supervisor doesn't approve the reimbursement request in a timely manner, the employee is under a lot of pressure, especially if the amount of money in question is large. By knowing which executives are inconsiderate about T&E reimbursements, the accounts payable department can show some mercy towards the employees involved. However, if the culprit is the employee and not the supervisor they should be given one chance and then no further exceptions.

21. One of the surest ways to blacken the reputation of the accounts payable department is to play favorites, issuing Rush checks and bending policy for "friends" while demanding

everyone else adhere to the guidelines. What's more, those departments that do favors for friends may not realize they are increasing the work for their staff. When it becomes known that certain people are getting special treatment, others will ask the favored person to bring their off-cycle requests to accounts payable. So, without realizing it, the departmental exception processing will go up.

22. Updating the accounts payable policy and procedures manual and T&E policy is hard work and tends not to get done as often as it should. When they are not updated, they gradually come to not reflect actual practices. This is where special treatments tend to sneak in. Update and share regularly to avoid additional hassles.

23. and 24. By providing information purchasing can use to negotiate better contracts, you will earn both the respect and gratitude of the purchasing department.

25. Once again, providing information to your customers is the best way to avoid problems caused because they don't know what your policies are. A one-page newsletter is a great way to keep them in the loop. Including a survey or a joke or something to engage them is a great way to ensure they'll read it each time it is issued.

So how'd you do? Did you get a few ideas on how to tweak your current processes? **DIYAP**

Best Practice Advice: Master Vendor File

The master vendor file is often the proverbial unwanted stepchild in certain organizations, stuck away and completely ignored. Others know they should pay attention to it, but somehow there is always something more pressing so it gets pushed to the back burner. And, let's face it, proper master vendor practices can be a royal pain when you are trying to get something done quickly. However, ignoring your master vendor file issues is no longer an option; it's likely to get you in hot water with your auditors and will definitely get you dinged in a Sarbanes-Oxley audit.

Importance

Why make such a big deal about the master vendor file? It's this simple: the better your master vendor file practices are the less likely you are to experience duplicate payments and fraud. And *everyone* knows neither of these is acceptable.

We should also point out that if you use the best practices discussed here, cleaning up the master vendor file will be much easier since you won't have introduced duplicate entries and other errors.

And finally, we have a warning, something you probably instinctively know but have pushed onto the far recesses of your mind. If you've never cleaned up your master vendor file, the first time is likely to be a nightmare. On the bright side, once you have gotten it done the first time, subsequent cleansings will be easier.

Master Vendor File Best Practices

The following are best practices as they relate to the master vendor file. As you can see they conform with other generally accepted best practices for your accounting and accounts payable operations.

1) Responsibility for the master vendor file can be in accounts payable, purchasing, or some other accounting department. The important point is that the person(s) responsible not have the authority to authorize a purchase, approve an invoice, or have anything to do with issuing the payment. For smaller organizations this often requires that the master vendor file reside outside accounts payable and/or purchasing.

2) Access to the master vendor file for purposes of adding or updates is limited to those with responsibility for the files.

3) A form should be created for updates and should not only be completed by the person requesting the addition/change but also signed off on by someone at a higher level and the forms filed.

4) Under no circumstances should passwords for the master vendor file be shared. In some organizations this is a firing offense as it completely negates other controls and makes it impossible to tell who made what changes.

5) Strict naming conventions should be used for entering data. These should conform to conventions used:

For entering invoice data, especially the vendor name

For creation of invoice numbers for invoices without invoice numbers

If these are not adhered to for every single entry into the master vendor file, duplicates will easily slip though.

6) The master vendor file should be cleansed at least annually although more frequently is a good idea for larger organizations. Some organizations do it every two years and while this is certainly better than never, once a year is preferable.

7) Deactivate inactive vendors, don't purge them. You never know when you will need the information to research a vendor claim. Therefore, purging is a big no-no.

8) Periodically, run a report showing the daily changes made to the master vendor file since your last report. In an ideal world this would be done daily but weekly or monthly is probably more realistic. The report should be given to a high-level executive for review. The main purpose of this routine is to serve as a deterrent to employees thinking about playing games with the master vendor file. It should also highlight questionable activity for further investigation.

Use these master vendor file best practices and see your duplicate payments plummet! It's fraud deterrent capabilities are a great side benefit. **DIYAP**

Best Practice Advice: 8 Simple Tactics to Reduce Stress in the AP/ Purchasing Relationship

The Felix-and-Oscar metaphor can sometimes be ascribed to the accounts payable and purchasing relationship. Sadly I'm afraid in this Odd Couple comparison, accounts payable comes off playing the role of Felix, the nitpicking neatnick always insisting things be done in a certain way. Meanwhile purchasing appears as the careless, messy Oscar forgetting deadlines and neglecting to fill out purchase orders completely—if at all. And as with Felix and Oscar, the accounts payable/purchasing divergent personalities often end in conflict.

While there are those accounts payable/purchasing relationships that have no need for a relationship counselor, the majority could use a few visits with a trained professional. In fact, there are a few that could use numerous visits. Recognizing that such counseling in not likely to take place, we've identified eight tactics that are likely to improve the relationship.

1. Be careful how you talk to the purchasing staff especially when there is a disagreement. It's easy when there is a problem to start the finger-pointing game. Go to great lengths to avoid accusations. I realize this is easier said than done, especially when the purchasing associate is proclaiming that he sent back an invoice to accounts payable weeks before he actually did. Still, by keeping the temperature of these conversations ratcheted down, you'll help the relationship in the long run.

2. Have a walk-a-mile-in-my-shoes day. Invite the purchasing associates who give you the biggest headaches to visit accounts payable and shadow one of the better team members for half a day. Save the problematic invoices submitted by this individual for processing while they are visiting. Let them see the problems they cause, keeping in mind the advice in item number one!

3. Have a walk-a-mile-in-***their***-shoes day. Fair's fair. If purchasing spends some time with accounts payable, AP should reciprocate and spend a day or half a day shadowing one of their professionals. Ideally, each processor should spend some time in purchasing so they can get an understanding of the problems the other side faces. By seeing what purchasing has to deal with accounts payable associates may be a little more understanding of issues when they arise.

4. Take your purchasing manager to lunch. Get away from the office and the workload and the hassle. Enjoy a meal discussing work only at the end of the meal. By getting to know the manager as a person first and business associate second, you'll stand a better chance of having a cordial relationship with the department.

5. Invite the purchasing staff to a potluck lunch—with AP bringing all the food. If each person brings a dish, perhaps their specialty, the two groups can have a little fun together. At this event, it is not necessary to discuss work at all. In fact, you might call the get together (no, don't gag) "Purchasing Appreciation Day."

6. In many organizations, accounts payable has access to data that purchasing needs. Typically this revolves around the total spend in various areas. Armed with this information, purchasing is in a good position to negotiate better contracts for the organization. Find out what it is that would help them the most and then run the reports they need to make their negotiating a little easier. This will enable them to deal from a position of strength rather than guessing what the company spent the prior year on a particular item.

7. Give purchasing marketplace intelligence you stumble across. Most often this will come to accounts payable when an invoice comes in with a lower price for an item than is on the purchase order. This can mean that the vendor is offering the product at a lower price than it is selling it to your company. Give this information to purchasing so they can use it in their negotiations.

8. As a sign of good faith, give them a get-out-of–jail-free card allowing them one rush check without a hassle. Some professionals who use this approach report that the cards never get used. Purchasing holds on to them waiting for that life-or-death occasion—which never comes. A few report a decrease in rush checks using this technique.

These are just a few things you can do to smooth some rough spots in the accounts payable/ purchasing relationship. Try one or two and you might be surprised to find out how a few kind gestures can pay off in a big way. **DIYAP**

Payments

- ♦ Payment Control Diagnostic
- ♦ ACH Diagnostic
- ♦ Identifying Problems that Can Be Eliminated with e-Payments" Diagnostic
  - ¨ P-card Missed Opportunity Diagnostic
- ♦ ACH Fraud
- ♦ Convincing Management to Make ACH Payments
- ♦ ¨ Best Practice Advice Payments Made Outside the Normal AP Process: A Control Disaster Waiting to Happen
- ♦ Best Practice Advice: Starting an ACH Payment Program
- ♦ Best Practice Advice: How An e-Payment Program Can Improve Your Bottom Line

Payment Control Diagnostic

As the accounts payable function gets increasingly sophisticated and the number of ways a payment can be made grows so does the "opportunity" for duplicate and erroneous payments. This diagnostic is designed to help you analyze your potential payment weaknesses. Let's see how good your processes are!

Overall

- Do you limit the payment type to one per vendor (i.e. only pay with checks, p-cards, ACH or wire)? ___ Yes ___ No
- Are your payment type limitations shown in your master vendor file? ___ Yes ___ No
- Do you periodically check to make sure all your wire transfers were not made a second time using a different payment vehicle? ___ Yes ___ No
- Does HR immediately notify accounts payable whenever someone leaves the organization? ___ Yes ___ No
- When AP is notified of an employee departure is the bank immediately notified if the person was a signer on the checking account? ___ Yes ___ No

Rush Payments

- Do you require complete backup for each rush payment? ___ Yes ___ No
- Is the PO closed (if there is one)? ___ Yes ___ No
- Is the receiving document extinguished? ___ Yes ___ No
- Is the applicable invoice number entered? ___ Yes ___ No
- Is the three-way match completed before the payment is made? ___ Yes ___ No
- Do you insist all rush payments be made by ACH instead of by check? ___ Yes ___ No

Wire Transfer

- Are you certain this has not been paid with a check or ACH? ___ Yes ___ No
-
- Are you certain this will not be paid in the future with a check or ACH? ___ Yes ___ No
- If there is an invoice associated with this payment, has the invoice number been entered as part of the transaction? ___ Yes ___ No
- Has the associated PO been closed, if there is one? ___ Yes ___ No
- Has the associated receiving document been extinguished, if there was one? ___ Yes ___ No

ACH

- Have you completed the three-way match? _ __ Yes ___ No
- Has the associated PO been closed, if there is one? ___ Yes ___ No
- Has the associated receiving document been extinguished, if there was one? ___ Yes ___ No
- When you receive change of account notifications from existing vendors, do you call a contact whose information you already have on hand to confirm the accuracy of the change? ___ Yes ___ No

P-cards

- Do you get Level 3 Data and check it closely? ___ Yes ___ No
- Do you require a supervisor to review all p-card charges and approve them? ___ Yes ___ No
- Do you use MCC restrictions? ___ Yes ___ No
- Do you have dollar limits set on all your cards consistent with the needs of the card holder, not his or her position within the company? ___ Yes ___ No
- Do you periodically get the employee list from HR and run it against your cardholder list to identify any cardholders who may have left the company? ___ Yes ___ No
- When AP is notified of an employee departure if the employee had a p-card, is the bank immediately notified and the card cancelled? ___ Yes ___ No

Payments from Statements

- If you pay a vendor based on statements, is the ability to pay an invoice submitted by this vendor blocked? ___ Yes ___ No
- If the ability to pay invoices is not blocked, do you periodically check to make sure no invoices have been paid? ___ Yes ___ No
- Do you limit the number of vendors paid from statements to a very few, ideally those who submit numerous low-dollar invoices? ___ Yes ___ No

Explanation of the Payment Control Diagnostic Responses

Clearly the correct answer to each of the questions is Yes. It is unlikely that more than a handful of our readers will actually have a positive response to every question. That being said, take the opportunity to investigate your processes where a negative reply was given to see if you can amend them to incorporate the recommended best practice.

If you can't, and we fully expect that to happen some of the time, devise other safeguards to make up for the weakness. For example, if you are not in the habit of entering an invoice number for Rush checks (because no invoice is available) regularly check your Rush checks issued against your regular check run to determine if that Rush check inadvertently created a duplicate. **DIYAP**

The ACH Diagnostic

1) Do you have detailed written procedures for your ACH program and include them in the accounts payable policy and procedures manual? ___ Yes ___ No

2) Do your ACH procedures mirror you check procedures? ___ Yes ___ No

3) Do your ACH procedures integrate strong internal controls throughout the process? ___ Yes ___ No

4) Do you check for duplicate payments made using other payment methodologies, i.e. paper check, T&E and p-card. Ideally every organization should be paid using one and only one payment mechanism? ___ Yes ___ No

5) Do you make sure receivers and POs are extinguished just as they would be if a paper check was the payment mechanism? ___ Yes ___ No

6) Do you put ACH blocks on all accounts where ACH activity will not be allowed? ___ Yes ___ No

7) Do you use ACH filters on those accounts where ACH debit activity will be allowed? ___ Yes ___ No

8) Do you have daily bank account reconciliations done on all accounts where ACH debits are permitted? Even better, reconcile all bank accounts on a daily basis? ___ Yes ___ No

9) Do you use a separate PC for all your online banking activities and do not use the computer for anything else? ___ Yes ___ No

10) Do you keep up to date on the latest information regarding fraud protection products offered by your financial institution and new frauds being perpetrated by crooks? ___ Yes ___ No

Explanation of the ACH Diagnostic Responses

Again, clearly the correct responses are all Yes. This is an area that is changing rapidly. What works today, may or may not work tomorrow. The crooks in this arena are getting increasingly sophisticated—and they are targeting accounts payable. What's more; when it comes to ACH or electronic payment fraud, it doesn't matter whether you are making electronic payments or not. Everyone is a target. It is critical that every organization take the appropriate steps to protect itself. **DIYAP**

How Many Ways Can An e-Payment Program Help Your Organization?

If someone were to make a list of all the petty problems that typically plague an accounts payable department, the list would probably go on for pages. Interestingly, paying electronically eliminates a good many problems.

The "Identifying Problems that Can Be Eliminated with e-Payments" Diagnostic

1) Does your organization issue more than a few Rush (ASAP) checks? ____ Yes ____ No

2) Do you have more than a few uncashed checks? ____ Yes ____ No

3) Does your staff spend time following up on uncashed checks? ____ Yes ____ No

4) Does your organization end up reporting and remitting more than a few dollars in unclaimed property to the states? ____ Yes ____ No

5) Has your process for issuing paper checks become so paper and people intensive, it requires several staffers to manage? ___ Yes ____ No

6) Could these people be assigned to more value add work? ___ Yes ___ No

7) Is your organization having a headcount reduction? ____ Yes ____ No

8) Is your accounts payable department being forced to take on additional work without being given additional headcount or budget? ____ Yes ____ No

9) Does your organization have trouble earning all the early payment discounts it is entitled to? ____ Yes ____ No

10) Is your accounts payable staff continually harangued by requisitioners who want their checks returned to them instead of being put in the mail? ___Yes ___ No

11) Is your organization looking for a better way to manage cash flow? ___ Yes ___ No

12) Are your suppliers starting to ask to be paid electronically? ___ Yes ____ No

13) Are you looking to eliminate some process work to free staffers up for work that adds value to the organization? ___ Yes ___ No

14) Are your bank reconciliations taking too much time because of all the un-cashed checks? ___ Yes ___ No

15) Do your vendors complain about checks taking too long to get to them, even after you know they've been mailed? ___ Yes ___ No

16) Does your staff spend much time looking for information about checks that have already been mailed but not received by the vendor? ___ Yes ___ No

17) Do your authorized signers take too long to put that second signature on the checks and return them for mailing? ___ Yes ___ No

18) Do you suspect some of the extra time being spent by authorized signers is simply be-

cause they are looking to see what other departments are spending not because they are verifying transactions? _____ Yes ____ No

19) Does your staff spend an inordinate amount of time collating backup for checks going out for signature and then separating the backup before the checks are mailed? ____ Yes ____ No

20) Do you think your organization spends too much money on having its checks printed? ____ Yes ____ No

Total _______ Yes _______ No

A Discussion of the "Identifying Problems that Can Be Eliminated with e-Payments" Diagnostic

Clearly every Yes on the diagnostic represents an opportunity to fix a problem by instituting an e-payment program or expanding an existing one. However before you can go down that road there is one other important question to ask yourself:

Does your organization have good up-front controls? If the answer is affirmative you are all set.

But, if your up-front controls are not as strong as they should be an errors are uncovered and fixed during the check production cycle then e-payments should be the second step in your problem elimination process. The first step has to be getting the appropriate controls in place. For without those strong controls you may end up paying more than a few invoices twice as well as creating a whole other set of problems for the organization.

But assuming you've gotten the up-front controls issue in order, let's take a look at why e-payments will help with the twenty problems we've identified.

1. By paying electronically, there is no longer any reason to have a Rush check. Companies who go this route have also seen a decline in the number of rush requests, especially if they are paying two to five times a week.
2. Un-cashed checks, if handled correctly, are a real time waster in accounts payable. They require tedious follow up and sometimes reissuing a check. With electronic payments, there is no such thing as an un-cashed check.
3. And if the payment should bounce back, the follow up is much less cumbersome.
4. With electronic payments there is much less to report and remit as unclaimed property to the states.
5. Staff is a valuable commodity. As much as feasibly possible, they are best utilized on work other than issuing checks.
6. Same as above.
7. A headcount reduction translates into fewer people to do the same work. This is an ideal time to move to electronic payments, which require less human interface.

8. Same as above. When additional work is being undertaken without adding staff, electronic payments are one nifty way to handle the increased workload.

9. Early payment discounts are extremely valuable to any organization. If the organization is having trouble earning them, electronic payments might be the answer. Editor's note: If you agree to pay electronically renegotiate the payment terms and see if you can get a few extra days.

10. Returning checks to requisitioners is a real poor practice for numerous reasons including it demonstrates poor internal controls. By eliminating the paper check you eliminate the problem.

11. When it comes to managing cash flow, electronic payments are worth their weight in gold. You know exactly when they will hit. There is no guessing the way there is with checks.

12. By agreeing to pay suppliers who to ask to be paid electronically you should be improving vendor relations.

13. Any time you have a task that adds value to the organization and you can free staff from clerical task, you are ahead of the game. Freeing them from the collating and separating of backup associated with paper checks is just what the doctor ordered.

14. Bank reconciliations are important but often take too much time because of all the outstanding checks. By eliminating paper checks you make the bank reconciliation process go much quicker.

15. Whether vendors complaining about checks taking too long to get to them, even after you know they've been mailed have a legitimate complaint or not, electronic payments does away with this issue.

16. Calls to accounts payable from vendors looking for information about checks that have already been mailed but not received are a necessary part of the accounts payable function. However, they are tedious and don't add any value – and go away when electronic payments are used.

17. Authorized signers who take too long to put that second signature on the checks and return them for mailing are an ongoing problem in a few organizations. If you didn't have to rely on them, the problem would disappear. This is why it is critical to get your upfront controls in place.

18. Same as above and you don't have to speculate on what they are doing with the checks for so long.

19. Again, freeing the staff from the task of getting checks in the envelope for mail will make your accounts payable department more efficient and productive.

20. When all other reasoning fails, look at the bottom line. That is something most management teams will pay attention to. Electronic payments cost a lost less than paper checks and today, everyone is interested in the bottom line!

Are you convinced? Are you ready to eliminate some of these problems from your accounts payable department? We certainly hope so. **DIYAP**

P-cards: Are You Missing Opportunities to Make Your Payment Function More Efficient?

Most professionals managing the accounts payable function are continually looking for ways to make the function more efficient. P-cards provide the answer to a myriad of problems. Whether you currently have a program or are considering one, our diagnostic quiz on page 11 will help you identify opportunities where p-cards could smooth out a bumpy payment road.

P-card Opportunity Diagnostic

1. Are you issuing too many 1099s for payments under $10,000? ___ Yes _____ No

2. Are you cutting checks for more than a few payments under $100 each year? ___ Yes _____ No

3. Do you have a petty cash box that you'd like to get rid of? ___ Yes _____ No

4. Does your staff spend far too much time administering, reconciling and reimbursing the petty cash box? ___ Yes _____ No

5. Do your organization's employees have a large number of subscriptions requiring managerial approval before renewal? ___ Yes _____ No

6. Is your organization actively looking to increase its rebate from its current program? ___ Yes _____ No

7. Are you concerned that some of the charges being put through on T&E cards for non-travel and entertainment items are not appropriate? ? ___ Yes _____ No

8. Are you looking for a way to efficiently reimburse maintenance staff for low-cost items they routinely purchase for their repair work? ___ Yes _____ No

9. Do you have a problem getting funds to employees who handle crises for you on the road, i.e. repair folks after tornadoes and hurricanes? ___ Yes _____ No

10. Are you under pressure to reduce the AP staff or take on more work without increasing staff? ? ___ Yes _____ No

Total ______ Yes _______No

Tabulate your responses as indicated above. Then turn the page to read a discussion of the responses.

A Discussion of the Now's P-card Opportunity Best Practices Results

As you may have deduced, the larger the number of yes responses you had, the greater your opportunity to use p-cards to improve your payment operations. Let's take a look at how each of the tactics work.

1) As you may be aware, starting in 2011, card issuers are responsible for issuing 1099s for payments made on cards. By pushing activity to your card programs, you will reduce the number of 1099s and subsequent B-Notices you have to deal with.

2) P-cards are the ideal solution for low-dollar payments. Investigate all low-dollar checks to determine if those payments are candidates for p-cards.

3) P-cards are also a solution for those looking to dump those productivity-sucking petty cash boxes.

4) Same as above.

5) Putting a p-card in the hands of the accounts payable manager or one of your supervisors is an ideal way to pay for subscriptions for the entire company.

6) Clearly, the only way to increase the rebate from your current program is to increase activity on the card. Those who do not currently have a card program should be aware that if you put sufficient activity on the card, the issuer will give you a rebate based on activity. Occasionally you will be able to increase that rebate by paying your credit card bill two or three weeks early.

7) Many organizations are concerned about purchases at gambling casinos and other similar activities. By putting Merchant Category Code (MCC) restrictions on the card, you can limit this type of activity. Be aware though, that this is not a perfect solution. Organizations that put T&E activity on the card and then send employees to conferences that happen to be held at a casino, sometimes run into trouble with this tactic. You can make exceptions, you just need to know about them in advance and alert the bank.

8) Cards with low-dollar limits are the perfect solution for those organizations that need to put a few dollars in the hands of maintenance or repair crews. This enables them to effectively get their job done without running a petty cash box or other cumbersome reimbursement processes.

9) Limits on cards can be adjusted as needed. So getting funds to employees who handle crises for you on the road, i.e. repair folks after tornadoes and hurricanes, is simple for those organizations that have given their employees cards. Of course, you need someone in the home office on call ready to turn the switch and contact the card issuer to increase limits. It doesn't happen automatically.

Many organizations are still under financial strains and pressure all departments to reduce staff or take on more work without increasing staff. P-cards provide a solution to that issue for the accounts payable function. **DIYAP**

Could Your Organization Be the Next Victim of ACH Fraud?

Unfortunately many professionals believe that since they don't make ACH payments their organization is not at risk. This is absolutely not true. Even those who understand the risks don't always keep up. The frauds in this arena are changing rapidly and if you don't stay on top of this issue you could find your organization on the wrong end of the game. Use AP Now's ACH Fraud Prevention/Detection diagnostic below to see how good a job your organization has done at protecting itself.

1. Have you set up a separate PC to be used only for online banking activity and nothing else? ___ Yes ___ No
2. Do you reconcile your bank accounts daily? ___ Yes ___ No
3. Do you limit your ACH debit activity to one or two bank accounts? ___ Yes ___ No
4. Are your ACH credits initiated out of one or two bank accounts? ___ Yes ___ No
5. Have you put ACH Blocks on all accounts where you do not want ACH activity to be initiated? ___ Yes ___ No
6. Have you put ACH filters on those accounts where you will permit ACH activity for certain parties? ___ Yes ___ No
7. Have you instructed all your staff to be careful about opening attachments to emails – even if they appear to come from legitimate third parties? ___ Yes ___ No
8. Have you instructed all your staff to be careful about clicking on links in emails – even if they appear to come from legitimate third parties? ___ Yes ___ No
9. Do you keep up-to-date on all new frauds? ___ Yes ___ No
10. Do you keep up-to-date on all new fraud prevention and detection products offered by your bank? ___ Yes ___ No
11. Do you get good contact information for your master vendor file when you set up new vendors? ___ Yes ___ No
12. Do you regularly update the contact information in your master vendor file? ___ Yes ___ No
13. When you receive letters or emails from vendors notifying you of a change of a Remit-to address, do you verify that with the vendor before making the change? ___ Yes ___ No
14. When you receive letters or emails from vendors notifying you of a change of a bank account, do you verify that with the vendor before making the change? ___ Yes ___ No
15. Do you review your positive pay rejects to see if there are any changes in the level of activity? ___ Yes ___ No
16. Do you regularly update the anti-virus software on all computers used in accounts pay-

able? ___ Yes ___ No

17. When an employee with payment responsibilities leaves the organization do you immediately cut off his/her access and notify the bank to terminate their access?
___ Yes ___ No

18. Do you immediately notify your bank when you spot an unauthorized ACH transaction?
___ Yes ___ No

19. Do you have someone checking your bank accounts on days when the company is closed but the banks open? ___ Yes ___ No

20. Do you insist that all staff who work with ACH activity take at least five consecutive days off from work and have someone else perform their tasks while they are absent?
___ Yes ___ No

Total _______ Yes ________ No

Discussion of the Best Practice Response to the ACH Fraud Prevention/Detection Checklist

Clearly, the best answer to each of the issues presented on the prior pages is yes. Let's take a look at the reasoning behind each one.

1. A separate PC to be used only for online banking activity and nothing else is the absolute best way to protect your organization from an account hijacking. It deprives fraudsters of the opportunity to grab your banking passwords and user IDs needed to perpetrate a corporate account takeover. Given the low cost of a PC, there is really no excuse for any organization not to follow this piece of advice. Yes, it is a little bit inconvenient to have to move to another computer to handle banking; but given the alternative, it is an inconvenience that should be tolerated.

2. Reconciling bank accounts every day will put you in the best position to notice unauthorized transactions and notify your bank. Since you only have 24 hours to do that, daily reconciliations are mandatory for those who have not put ACH blocks on their accounts.

3. Limiting ACH debit activity to one or two bank account limits the accounts that have to be closely monitored on a very regular basis.

4. Limiting the accounts where you initiate ACH credits to one or two bank accounts makes it easier to manage ACH activity as well as monitor for fraud.

5. Putting ACH Blocks on all accounts where you do not want ACH activity to be initiated is the best way to prevent crooks from creating debits against your account. This is especially important for those who use positive pay as crooks now routinely represent positive pay rejects as ACH debits.

6. Putting ACH filters on those accounts where you will permit ACH activity for certain parties is the best way to make sure that only those authorized to debit your account will

actually do so.

7. Instructing all your staff to be careful about opening attachments to emails – even if they appear to come from legitimate third parties – will limit your chances of being hit with malware that facilitates an account hijacking.

8. Instructing all your staff to be careful about clicking on links in emails – even if they appear to come from legitimate third parties – will limit your chances of being hit with malware that facilitates an account hijacking.

9. New frauds in the ACH arena, as well as variations of old ones, are developing rapidly. Keeping up-to-date on all new frauds is a critical component of protecting your organization.

10. Similarly, keeping up-to-date on all new fraud prevention and detection products offered by your bank is important so you evaluate and select the best fraud prevention/ detection strategy for your organization.

11. Many organizations overlook the step of getting good contact information for their master vendor file when they set up new vendors. Then when there is a problem, they don't know who to call. These problems come in the form of a fraudster posing as the vendor. It is becoming critical that good contact information, in addition to the Remit-to address be collected when the vendor is set up in the master vendor file.

12. Once you obtain the contact information, it must be regularly updated or it will fast become outdated.

13. Whenever you receive letters or emails from vendors notifying you of a change of a Remit-to address, it is critical that request be verified with the vendor before making the change. This is just one way crooks pose as vendors to get money they are not entitled to.

14. Whenever you receive letters or emails from vendors notifying you of a change of a bank account, it is also critical you verify that request with the vendor before making the change.

15. By reviewing your positive pay rejects to see if there are any changes in the level of activity, you will be able to determine if anything unusual is going on. And by unusual we mean if someone has gotten access to your banking information and is using it for nefarious purposes.

16. Regularly update the anti-virus software on all computers used in accounts payable is a non-negotiable tactic given the heightened concerns about electronic payment fraud.

17. Whenever an employee with payment responsibilities leaves the organization, immediately cut off his/her access and notify the bank to terminate their access. Most employees are honest but you don't want to get taken by the one or two who are not.

18. It is critical that you immediately notify your bank when you spot an unauthorized ACH transaction as businesses only have 24 hours to advise the bank, if they want to be assured of getting their funds returned.

19. Someone should check your bank accounts on days when the company is closed but

the banks open. The 24 hour clock discussed above is ticking whether your company is open for business or not.

20. By insisting that all staff who work with ACH activity take at least five consecutive days off from work and having someone else perform their tasks while they are absent you will hopefully uncover any ongoing fraud. In that time.

So how'd you do? If you did not answer yes to any of the issues, don't wait to fix them. You don't want to be in the position of locking the barn door after the horse has been stolen. **DIYAP**

Making the Case: Convincing Management to Pay Electronically

Is your organization part of the group that is still not paying at least some of its vendors electronically? Have you been having trouble framing your case to get management approval? Use the Best Practice checklist below to help you get started.

1. Have you compared the out-of-pocket costs for issuing a check versus issuing an electronic payment (ACH credit or debit)? ___ Yes ___ No

2. Have you pointed out the fact that there is little or no unclaimed property when paying electronically, relieving the staff of their due diligence in this regard as well as the reporting and remitting responsibilities? ___ Yes ___ No

3. Have you calculated the time saving on doing bank reconciliations as there are no outstanding payments as there are with paper checks? ___ Yes ___ No

4. Have you calculated the amount of time spent manually handling paper checks, including but not limited to collating, stuffing envelopes, getting a second signature if needed etc.? ___ Yes ___ No

5. Have you taken into consideration the improvement in vendor satisfaction when the money goes directly into their bank account instead of being 'lost in the mail'? ___ Yes ___ No

6. Have you contemplated requiring all Rush payments be made electronically, simplifying that whole process of payments made under pressure? ___ Yes ___ No

7. Have you pointed out that with electronic payments, the whole issue of requisitioners requesting checks be returned to them (a really poor internal control) is eliminated? ___ Yes ___ No

8. Have you considered using electronic payments via ACH as an alternative to costly wire transfers? ___ Yes ___ No

9. If you are storing paper checks, have you taken into account the space savings? ___ Yes ___ No

10. Have you pointed out that the Federal government is taking the lead and paying virtually everyone electronically? ___ Yes ___ No

A Discussion of the Responses

When making your case for a move to electronic payments, each of the items discussed is a clear benefit. So, address as many of them as you can. For the more you hit, the better your chance for getting a green light on an electronic payment program. Let's see why.

1. To be blunt, ACH payments are a lot cheaper than issuing a paper check. Even if you just look at the hard dollar costs like bank fees, printing charges and postage. With electronic payments, the last two costs don't apply.

2. The work associated with un-cashed checks and unclaimed property virtually disappears when paying electronically. This relieves the staff of their due diligence efforts as well as the reporting and remitting responsibilities.

3. Bank reconciliations are much easier as there are no outstanding payments as there are with paper checks.

4. Manual handling associated with paper checks, including but not limited to collating, stuffing envelopes, getting a second signature if needed etc. can eat up a lot of staff time without adding any real value to the transaction. With electronic payments most of it is eliminated.

5. Most vendors are amenable to having payments go directly into their bank account instead of being 'lost in the mail.' This can lead to improved vendor satisfaction and relations.

6. Rush checks are another non-value add task for the accounts payable staff. However, from time to time they are a necessity. By requiring all Rush payments be made electronically, you simplify the whole process of payments made under pressure.

7. Returning checks to requisitioners not only adds non-value add work to the accounts payable function, it is a very poor internal control. While occasionally it may be necessary, more often than not, the reason for the return request is not a good one. The whole issue of returning checks to requisitioners can be eliminated by paying electronically.

8. Wire transfers are electronic payments but making payments via wire is expensive. Considered using electronic payments via ACH as an alternative to these costly transfers.

9. One of the benefits of any digital or electronic project is the elimination of paper documents and thus the need for space to store those documents. If you are storing paper checks or copies of those checks, there will be some space savings with the move to electronic payments. While this may not be as huge a savings as when invoices are imaged, every little bit helps.

10. It should be noted that the Federal government is taking the lead and paying virtually everyone electronically. If it's good enough for them, why isn't it good enough for your company? **DIYAP**

Best Practice Advice: Payments Made Outside the Normal AP Process: A Control Disaster Waiting to Happen

In many organizations, wire transfers were often made outside of accounts payable. Since these tend to be large dollar payments, frequently for items where an invoice is not prepared, there were few problems. This is not to say that duplicate payments never get made; they occasionally were. And, when they did they were doozies. As we move forward into the electronic payment arena, it appears that ACH payments are more than occasionally being initiated outside accounts payable. This can present a real problem under certain circumstances. When a reader wrote to ask about payments made via journal entry, we decided to investigate the issue.

"Seems that every company I have worked for has a habit of booking certain payments through a journal entry instead of having AP process it," she notes. She explains further. "Since AP does not process them, the W-9s and W-8 are not collected and there is not a clear audit trail of who is being paid. If I find out about these payments I will try to convince Treasury to let us run them through AP but they are not always forth coming on what they are booking. What are the best practices for handling these situations?"

Here's what we recommend.

- Monthly review all wire transfer and journal entry activity to ensure no duplicate payment was made. These transactions should be compared to check runs and ACH payments. This review should be done for 60-90 days after the wire. If a duplicate is found, identify the internal control weakness that permitted this and fix it.
- When the review is being conducted, associated PO and receiving documents should be extinguished (if they exist), if they were not when the payment was made.
- Work with your auditors to convince management that normal payment processes should be followed when any payment is made, regardless who makes it. We're not saying that all payments must be made in accounts payable. However, if other areas making payments are not following best practices and including strong internal controls, a case can be made for moving that activity to accounts payable.
- Given the attractiveness of ACH pricing compared to wire transfer pricing, propose that wire transfers be replaced with ACH transactions, especially if it is handled in accounts payable.
- Have a duplicate payment audit performed by a third party contingency firm. If no duplicates or other erroneous payments were made, you are probably in good shape. However, if there were a large number of duplicates, immediately start an investigation into why they occurred and fix the controls that allowed this. Sometimes a report from a third party showing problems when payments are not all made by one department is all that is needed to get those other payments back into accounts payable.

As we move into the electronic payment arena in greater numbers, the challenges facing accounts payable are likely to grow. By recognizing where the problems might occur, you will be well positioned to deal with them effectively for your organization. **DIYAP**

Best Practice Advice: Starting an ACH Payment Program

Without a doubt, at some point in the next decade, every organization will make at least part if not all of their payments electronically. Many have already started to do so. Others are considering programs now—or will be in the near future when an 800-pound-gorilla supplier insists on electronic payments. If you haven't yet started an electronic program, what follows is a look at some of the issues you should consider before launching one. Readers should note that they will sometimes hear ACH payments referred to as direct payments, a play on direct deposit of payroll.

Start with the Bank

The first place you need to go if you want to pay using ACH is to the bank where your checking account is. The bank officer assigned to your account should be able to put you in touch wit the right personnel in the bank. He or she will help you get set up and offer you some advice on converting vendors. Don't contact any vendor until you are comfortable with the process the bank suggests. You may have to make certain adjustments to your processes or accounting system and in all likelihood this will require technical support.

Depending on who has the relationship with the bank, it may be necessary to get treasury or accounting involved. Only when you have the banking, accounting, and IT concerns under control should you consider your first electronic payment.

Crawling before You Walk

A good way to get started, says a controller we spoke with, is to begin paying employee expense reimbursements by ACH. This will save money for the company (the cost of printing checks) and time for the employees (no need to make a trip to the bank to deposit reimbursement checks). Also, it will give the accounts payable department an opportunity to get used to the process. It should be an easy set up since payroll should have the direct deposit info on file so there is an opportunity to have a few "good wins" in the transition.

Once everyone is comfortable with the process, she advises, begin contacting your vendors and asking if it is possible to make payments electronically. This step should be taken with some care. Some who have contacted all their vendors at one time have learned the hard way— when the positive response was much higher than they anticipated—that they couldn't accommodate everyone at once.

The controller explains this can happen because most companies are happy to accept electronic payments, as it reduces their processing costs (no taking checks to the bank) and the funds received are verified (no bounced checks). ACH payments are typically free to receive, so they also avoid the processing costs charged by their bank and eliminate the "float".

The Cash Flow Impact

Our readers, warns the controller, should also consider that transitioning to ACH payments will have an impact on cash flow (no float) as the money will be withdrawn from their account typically within two days of initiating the transfer. Therefore, it's important that those doing cash flow forecasting be included in the ACH planning. More than one accounts payable manager has ended up with egg on his or her face after implementing what they thought was a great program only to have cash flow fall short of what was planned and management less than pleased with the outcome.

There is a relatively simple solution to this problem, although it will take some planning and management support. Many organizations renegotiate their payment terms to take an extra two or three days to make the transaction float neutral.

Auditors really like ACH payments, points out the controller, since there are no checks sitting around on someone's desk waiting to be mailed. She also notes that controllers are also happy due to fewer outstanding items on the bank reconciliation at the end of the month. Given the rough economic times many organizations currently face, do not down play the importance of cash flow.

Getting Vendor Information

An accounting manager we spoke with explained how he verifies bank information. "We require a copy of a cancelled check, a copy of a deposit ticket or ACH instructions on company letterhead maybe with an office signature to verify information," he says.

This step is taken to insure that no one inserts their own bank information. Some organizations will only take the voided check or deposit ticket. The opportunity for fraud is high here, although to be honest there have only been a limited number of reports of this type of fraud.

Other Considerations

There are other issues to take into consideration when starting a program. They include:

Be careful who you invite. If you have any thoughts of paying a particular vendor with a credit card in the future, do not invite them to participate in your program. It will be difficult to convert them from ACH to p-card, so better to avoid the issue completely.

Depending on the accounting system in use, it may still be possible to do a separate "check run" in AP for electronic payments so that the record-keeping is easier. If the accounting system in use does not allow for this, then the reader should consider how these records will be kept.

Consider creating a FAQ brochure for vendors answering the most common questions. This preemptive approach can help overcome objections before they occur.

Once you have contacted all vendors, look for other ways to get vendors into your ACH program. One of the easiest is to insist that all rush payments will be made by ACH, not paper check. In many cases once they receive one payment electronically, they'll never want to go back to paper.

Concluding Thoughts

The Electronic Payments Network makes some information available online, although much of their advice is aimed at consumers rather than businesses. You can see what they have at www.electronicpayments.org/individuals/in.direct-payment.php

Whether or not you have a program now, electronic payments will play a big part in the payment world of the future. This is one of those areas everyone needs to learn about and master doing well. **DIYAP**

Best Practice Advice: How An e-Payment Program Can Improve Your Bottom line

Innovative professionals are finding additional ways to wring savings from their electronic payment initiatives and the bottom line improvements related to these initiatives are impressive. Most professionals reading this are well aware that moving payments from paper checks to electronic payments via the ACH will save them money, while improving their departmental efficiency. Most probably think the financial savings are related to the cost to send an ACH versus the cost of producing and mailing a check. And they are partially correct. But, that is just the first step. These savings pale in comparison to the financial improvements available through other techniques. This article discusses some of the tactics being used in some organizations that are adding real dollars to their organizations profitability.

Pricing Discounts

Occasionally, some suppliers will offer small pricing discounts or rebates to their customers who agree to pay them electronically. This is the best of all worlds for the customer. They get to pay with the least expensive payment mechanism while simultaneously getting a price reduction or rebate—both of which effectively increase the bottom line. The offer of such a savings has been more than enough to convince quite a few organizations to convert to electronic payments.

Like discounts offered for early payments, these incentives should be viewed positively and taken if at all feasible, assuming, of course that they make financial sense. Do the math if offered a pricing discount. However, keep in mind that usually this is a financial incentive you can't beat.

Keep in mind that practices such as this tend to run in industries. Thus, if you find one vendor offering a pricing discount for electronic payment, its competitors are also likely to offer the discount. If one of the market leaders offers the discount, your purchasing staff should be able to gain the same concession from the smaller players in the market. This is probably an area that should be approached with purchasing as a joint project, rather than alone without purchasing.

Renegotiating Payment Terms

Often when the topic of paying electronically is raised, management is reluctant because they perceive that they will lose the float benefits. Companies want to use this new technology yet are not willing to give up the few extra days of "float" can renegotiate their payment terms with vendors to make the transaction float neutral. This way neither party gains or loses by the transition to the new payment methodology.

When payments are made electronically the funds get into the supplier's bank account immediately and generally the vendor has use of good funds one day later. This is typically several days sooner than if the check had gone through the traditional printing and mailing cycle. Recognizing this fact, some use this information to entice vendors to accept payments electronically.

Should you take this tack? In an ideal world the answer is of course you should. But if vendors refuse to renegotiate the terms you may end up continuing paying them with paper checks. So the real answer is: it depends. If your company's primary goal is to get rid of the checks then the answer is to tread lightly on the float issue. If, on the other hand, cash flow is an issue for your firm then you may have to rethink how you address the terms question. Accounts payable managers should not make this decision in a vacuum. Management input is required when deciding how important float is in this equation.

Improved Terms vs. Pricing Discounts

Generally speaking, the improved payment terms offered to make a transaction float neutral translates into two or three days added to the terms. Occasionally, if a vendor is voraciously interested in getting paid electronically, it might offer an additional five days to make the transaction float neutral.

Pricing discounts on the other hand will generally be some fraction of one percent. Again, this is not a huge amount, unless you are talking about large invoices. However, it is found money that goes straight to the bottom line.

Although you should do the math if you are doubtful, generally speaking pricing discounts or rebates should be taken, if offered, before the slightly extended payment terms.

If approaching the vendor to ask for an incentive, start with the pricing discount and then move on to the renegotiated terms to make the transaction float neutral.

What if No Discounts or Renegotiated Terms Are Offered

Of course, this is an issue every organization has to wrestle with, especially if they really do want to pay everyone electronically. In an ideal world, begin by asking for a pricing discount. If turned down on that, request that payment terms be extended a few days to make the transaction float neutral. Since most organizations cannot convert everyone from paper to electronics overnight, focus on the groups that will offer something in return.

Once you have converted everyone who will offer something, move on to those who will give nothing in return.

If you are already paying electronically, you will be at a severe disadvantage in trying to get a vendor to offer a pricing discounts or renegotiate terms.

There is one last caveat. If your organization is focused on p-cards and rebates carefully evaluate vendors before offering them electronic payments. Once you are paying them electronically, they are not likely to want to be converted to p-cards unless the dollar amount is really small. **DIYAP**

Travel & Entertainment

- The T&E Policy Diagnostic
- T&E Expense Policies that Meet IRS Guidelines while Combatting Fraud
- Avoiding a T&E Fraud Debacle Debacle
- The T&E Receipts Issue
- Best Practice Advice: Seeing T&E as a Regulatory Issue
- Best Practice Advice: Sample T&E Best Practice Guidelines

The T&E Policy Diagnostic

It's really easy to go wrong when it comes to a corporate T&E policy. Just ask Thomas Coughlin, who resigned in March as Wal-Mart's vice chairman. The company has accused him of taking as much as $500,000 from unauthorized gift card transactions and fraudulent expense reports. So, how does a company with a balance sheet as strong as Wal-Mart's end up in such a mess? Without access to inside Wal-Mart information and policies we don't know. We do know, however, how to identify gaps in corporate T&E policies. The following diagnostic will help you determine if your organization is laying any T&E landmines.

1) Does your company have a formal written T&E policy, approved by management?
____Yes _____ No

Potential Issue: Without a formal written policy it is impossible to mandate policy and track individual compliance. You'll also run afoul of all Sarbanes-Oxley internal control requirements.

2) Has your company's T&E policy been updated within the last 12 months?
____Yes _____ No

Potential Issue: All policies as well as written manuals should be updated and reviewed at least annually if not more frequently. At a minimum, changes in per diems as well as the reimbursement rate for mileage should be updated to reflect market conditions.

3) Is everyone in the company—including the most senior officers—required to comply with the T&E policy? ____Yes _____ No

Potential Issue: Besides the fairness issue, the ability to monitor compliance goes right out the window if certain people are excluded. This should not be confused with differing policies for different groups of employees. For example, in some firms officers may fly first class while non-officer employees get coach seats.

4) Do you spot check T&E expense reimbursement requests instead of checking each report? _____Yes _____ No

Potential Issue: Verifying T&E reports is a time consuming task that adds little value. Not checking at all is an unattractive option too as travelers might get a little loose with their reporting if they thought no one was watching.

5) Does your organization offer cash advances? _____Yes _____ No

Potential Issue: While providing cash advances to employees might seem like a fair thing to do, it usually backfires on the employer. With no money out of their pockets many employees do not feel it necessary to file their T&E reports. However, if they need that reimbursement to pay the credit card bill most will feel a certain urgency when it comes to filing their reports.

Explanation of the Diagnostic Responses

With the exception of number five, the correct answer to all the questions is yes. While $500,000 is just a drop in the bucket to Wal-Mart the negative publicity associated with this alleged fraud is far more damaging. At a minimum, your T&E policy should incorporate the concepts discussed here. The days of being able to look the other way when someone violated T&E policy are fast coming to an end. Sarbanes-Oxley, corporate cost cutting initiatives, and an overriding desire to avoid negative press are forcing companies everywhere to implement the same types of stringent controls in their T&E programs as they do in other parts of their businesses. **DIYAP**

Do Your T&E Expense Policies Meet IRS Guidelines & Combat Fraud?

A good travel and entertainment (T&E) policy not only sets guidelines for employees traveling and/or entertaining on behalf of their organization, it should also protect a company against fraud and help ensure the company meets IRS guidelines for an accountable plan. Does your policy accomplish both those goals? Answer the following questions and then sum up the total positive and negative responses.

1. Do you require receipts for all expenditures over $75? (Note: Answer yes if you require receipts over a lower dollar level.) ____ Yes ____ No
2. If you use per-diems, do you use rates at or below the CONUS rates? ____ Yes ____ No
3. If you use per-diems above the CONUS rates, do you require documentation? ____ Yes ____ No
4. If you use per-diems above the CONUS rates, do you require the return of the excess? ____ Yes ____ No

5. If you use per-diems above the CONUS rates, do you report the excess on the employees' W-2? ___ Yes ___ No

6. Do your require employees to document attendees at business events paid for by your organization (names, company names, titles and business relationship)? ___ Yes ___ No

7. Do your require employees to document the business purpose of events paid for by your organization? ___ Yes ___ No

8. If you offer cash advances, do you require employees must account for their expenses within 60 days of when the expenses were incurred? ___ Yes ___ No

9. If you offer cash advances, do you require employees to return any excess reimbursement (cash advances) within 120 days after the expense was paid or incurred? ___ Yes ___ No

10. Do you reimburse mileage at or below the IRS optional mileage reimbursement level? ___ Yes ___ No

11. Do you mandate the use of a corporate credit card for all T&E expenditures? ___ Yes ___ No

12. Do you rely on something other than the boarding pass to verify a trip? ___ Yes ___ No

13. Does your organization have a written policy of Zero Tolerance for fraud or abuse? ___ Yes ___ No

14. Does your organization make managers responsible for the expense reimbursement reports they approve? ___ Yes ___ No

15. Is you T&E policy detailed and shared with all employees? ___ Yes ___ No

16. Does your organization mandate uniform enforcement of its T&E policy? ___ Yes ___ No

17. Do you require that the highest level employee at an event pay for it and put in for reimbursement? ___ Yes ___ No

18. Do you have a policy that prohibits an employee from approving expenditures for an event at which he or she was a participant? ___ Yes ___ No

19. Do you have a policy that prohibits the submission of an invoice as part of a T&E expense reimbursement request? ___ Yes ___ No

20. Do you have a process for tracking unused tickets? ___ Yes ___ No

Total _______ Yes ________ No

A Discussion of the Best Practice Responses to the AP Now IRS Compliant, Fraud Resistant T&E Policy Checklist

Of AP Now's quizzes where the best practice response is Yes for each of the questions. Some of the answers may be surprising so let's take a look at why the positive response was the best practice answer in each of these cases.

1. The IRS only requires receipts for all expenditures over $75? So, if you are collecting them for everything above $75 (or some lower dollar level) you are in compliance with IRS regs. However many organizations require documentation at a lower level as a way of ensuring policy compliance and making T&E fraud harder to perpetrate.
2. Using per-diems at or below the CONUS rates avoids a whole lot of accounting and red tape. If you are going to use per-diems, use the CONUS rates.
3. When you use per-diems above the CONUS rates, there are a number of additional accounting tasks you must do starting with requiring documentation.
4. When you use per-diems above the CONUS rates you must require the return of the excess if you don't want to have further problems.
5. When you use per-diems above the CONUS rates, you must report the excess unreturned amount on the employees' W-2.
6. In order to substantiate to the IRS a business expense you must have documented the attendees at business events paid for by your organization (names, company names, titles and business relationship)?
7. In order to substantiate to the IRS a business expense you must have your employees document the business purpose of events paid for by your organization.
8. Requiring that employees must account for their expenses within 60 days of when the expenses were incurred will help secure your accountable plan status. This guideline is quite generous and most best practice recommendations are for a shorter period.
9. Requiring that employees return any excess reimbursement (cash advances) within 120 days after the expense was paid or incurred will also help secure your accountable plan status. This guideline is quite generous and most best practice recommendations are for a shorter period.
10. Reimburse mileage at or below the IRS optional mileage reimbursement level avoids the ugly task of calculating the excess and including that amount on your employees' W-2.
11. Mandating the use of a corporate credit card for all T&E expenditures eliminates the "opportunity" for some employees to play games when charging expenses (mostly airline) for corporate travel.
12. Relying on something other than the boarding pass to verify a trip makes good sense since boarding passes are now printable at home.
13. Having a written policy of Zero Tolerance for fraud or abuse puts employees on notice that the organization takes fraud seriously and will not tolerate it.

14. Making managers responsible for the expense reimbursement reports they approve puts the organization one step closer to having managers actually review what they sign. If it is part of their yearend review, they may be less likely to just sign without looking at what they are signing.

15. A T&E policy that is detailed and shared with all employees is your first step towards eliminating fraud and abuse. With a written policy no one can claim they didn't realize the company wouldn't pay for an item.

16. Uniform enforcement of its T&E policy is one of the best ways to not only get compliance but to improve morale. When the policy is not enforced equally, employees are sometimes tempted to put through items not on the policy – especially when they see others being reimbursed for the same item.

17. Requiring that the highest level employee at an event pay for it and put in for reimbursement puts an end to the games employees sometimes play where the junior person puts in for a meal and the senior employee approves it. There have been numerous instances where weekly luncheons at expensive restaurants are put on the corporate tab. If there is a legitimate business reason for these events, there should be no problem getting the event approved by the more senior employee's supervisor. If that is a problem, then perhaps the meetings should be taking place in the office without that expensive meal.

18. A policy that prohibits an employee from approving expenditures for an event at which he or she was a participant avoids even the slightest appearance of impropriety. Similar to the discussion above, if the expense is legitimate, there should be no problem getting it approved.

19. There is no reason why an employee should pay a company invoice. When invoices are paid through T&E the chance of a duplicate payment skyrockets. Having a policy that prohibits the submission of an invoice as part of a T&E expense reimbursement request should put an end to that practice.

20. Unused tickets, especially in this age of paperless tickets create numerous headaches for organizations. Having a process for tracking unused tickets not only ensures the organization doesn't let the tickets go unused after paying for them, it also helps protect against an employee who might decide to use that ticket for personal travel. **DIYAP**

Does Your Travel & Entertainment Policy and Review Process Make It Easy for Crooks and Spendthrifts?

The T&E policy itself as well as how it is administered are two important ingredients in stopping the games employees play with their T&E expense reimbursement requests. The checklist will help you identify those areas where your policy and/or processes might benefit from some reengineering to assure no theft or flagrant spending happens on your watch.

AP Now's Avoiding a T&E Fraud Debacle Quiz

1. Do you spot check actual mileage against what the employee has submitted? ___ Yes ___ No

2. Do you do a close review of the receipts for cash expenditures? ___ Yes ___ No

3. Do you do a close review of any employee who submits numerous expense reimbursement requests for expenditures right below the receipt threshold? ___ Yes ___ No

4. Do you do any sort of checking to determine how many people actually participated in a business meal? ___ Yes ___ No

5. Do you check to determine if any of your employees have been adding gift cards to restaurant bills when entertaining clients? ___ Yes ___ No

6. If your policy forbids liquor, do you verify that no liquor was included on the expense reimbursement? _ __ Yes ___ No

7. When handwritten receipts are submitted do you check older expense reimbursement requests from the same employee checking for sequential numbers to ensure the receipts aren't being pulled from a pad the employee owns? ___ Yes ___ No

8. Are you certain that reimbursement requests for gifts are actually for items given to a customer or supplier and not kept by the employee? ___ Yes ___ No

9. Do you verify there is a business relationship for all expenditures for entertainment submitted by your employees? ___ Yes ___ No

10. Do you get credit cards (and p-cards) back from all departing employees? ___ Yes ___ No

11. Do you cancel the credit cards (and p-cards) for all departing employees? ___ Yes ___ No

12. Is your T&E policy detailed so there can be no misunderstanding on the part of your traveling employees? ___ Yes ___ No

13. If your organization does not reimburse for liquor is this spelled out in detail in your policy? ___ Yes ___ No

14. If your organization does not reimburse for movies in the room of traveling employees, is this spelled out in your policy? ___ Yes ___ No

15. Do you have a written policy identifying those circumstances where cabs should be utilized instead of renting a car? ___ Yes ___ No

16. If you do not use per diems, do you have written guidelines on how much an employee can reasonably spend for meals when traveling but not entertaining a client or supplier? ___ Yes ___ No

17. Are managers held accountable for the expense reports they approve? ___ Yes ___ No

18. Do you check reimbursements for meals and entertainment to make sure the highest ranking employee submitted the expense? ___ Yes ___ No

19. Is your T&E policy widely shared with all employees, including admins who might not travel but complete expense reimbursement reports for their bosses? ___ Yes ___ No

20. When a receipt for expense reimbursement shows a weekend date, do you question it? ___ Yes ___ No

Total ___ Yes _____ No

Turn the page for a discussion of the best practice responses.

A Discussion of the Best Answers to AP Now's Avoiding a T&E Debacle Quiz

Clearly, the ideal response to each question is yes. Questionable expense reimbursement requests can be a slippery slope. Once an employee has gotten away with one dubious item, the next time he or she is likely to push the envelope a little further. Let's take a look at the reasoning behind each one of these issues. .

1. Spot checking actual mileage against what the employee has submitted is the best way to make sure employees aren't playing games with their mileage. This is one of the oldest frauds with some employees routinely adding 100 miles to every trip. Some of the newer T&E software, such as InterplX's T&E ExpenseNet have a mileage validation tool built in.

2. A close review of the receipts for cash expenditures will help you determine whether the expenditure should have been included for reimbursement. Traveling employees have been known to submit reimbursement requests for all sorts of large bottles of toiletries. Only in a true emergency should the employee be putting in for those items in the first place.

3. Numerous expense reimbursement requests for expenditures right below the receipt threshold is a red flag. Often the employee isn't actually spending that money but rather something lower. If you appear to have an abuser, have a conversation with the employee, letting them know you are watching this issue. For this reason many companies have dropped their receipt requirement level to $5.

4. Checking to determine how many people actually participated in a business meal is not usually done. However, if you suspect there is a problem, change your policy to require the itemized receipt for all meals. Then check those receipts to determine how many main courses were ordered.

5. Similarly, if restaurant receipts seem high and you suspect employees of adding gift cards to restaurant bills when entertaining clients, change your policy to require the itemized receipt for all meals.

6. If your policy forbids liquor, change your policy to require the itemized receipt for all meals. This can be used to verify that no liquor was included on the expense reimbursement. This issue is critical to those dependent on grants that specifically exclude the reimbursement for liquor.

7. Handwritten receipts are another red flag. Sometimes they are legitimate but fewer and fewer businesses are using them. Check older expense reimbursement requests from the same employee checking for sequential numbers to ensure the receipts aren't being pulled from a pad the employee owns, if you get more than the occasional hand written receipt.

8. The spotlight on this issue occurred several years ago when a high level executive at one of the major retailers took gift cards intended for employee bonuses and used them for personal purchases. After that, the need to make sure reimbursement requests for gifts are actually for items given to the intended recipient became clear. One way to do this is to insist the items are mailed or delivered to the recipients' places of business. You can check this by looking at the delivery slips or order confirmations. Many organizations chose to rely on the employee's honesty rather than do any checking, especially when only a few items are purchased.

9. Verify there is a business relationship for all expenditures for entertainment submitted by your employees is a simple task. According to IRS rules, it should be included in the documentation the employee supplies. Employees submitting for expenses spent enter-

taining those with whom no business relationship exists could be endangering the organization's accountable plan status.

10. Getting credit cards (and p-cards) back from all departing employees not only makes good sense, it prevents the employees from using the cards when they no longer have the right to do so.

11. Canceling the credit cards (and p-cards) for all departing employees ensures cards are not used when they shouldn't be.

12. A detailed T&E policy prevents any misunderstanding on the part of your traveling employees?

13. Spelling out what will not be reimbursed is critical to avoid misunderstandings or the infamous "no one ever told me" excuses. It is especially important for liquor if the organization is dependent on grants which prohibit reimbursing for liquor.

14. Similarly, if your organization does not reimburse for movies in the room of traveling employees, spell it out in your policy to avoid unpleasantness.

15. Some travelers automatically rent a car whenever traveling. This can be a costly option, especially in big cities. Let me give you a simple example. Say an employee is going to a conference in midtown New York City. The daily parking rate at the hotel is $51 and they are staying five nights. They simply drive to the hotel, park the car and then when they leave, pick the car up and drive back to the airport. Simply parking the car – before tax, tip, car rental, tolls, gas etc. exceeds $250. Do I have to write anything else to convince you that a cab makes more sense in this situation – even if the cab ride were $100 each way (which it isn't)? You can check the cost of parking a car (before tax and tip) at the hotel by looking at the hotel website. Simple guidelines about when a car rental is appropriate will prevent this type of over expenditure.

16. Just because your organization does not use per diems, doesn't mean you shouldn't provide written guidelines on how much an employee can reasonably spend for meals when traveling but not entertaining a client or supplier. Let's face it; most employees will opt for filet mignon when offered that or a hamburger. And just because the company reimburses for liquor, doesn't mean a $200 bottle of wine should be ordered. Avoid unpleasant encounters of this type by providing broad guidelines.

17. Making managers accountable for the expense reports they approve is one of the best ways to put an end to T&E shenanigans. It means they will have to look closely at their subordinates' expense reimbursement requests and not automatically sign whatever is put in front of them.

18. Check reimbursements for meals and entertainment to make sure the highest ranking employee submitted the expense. Otherwise, you may find all sorts of questionable expenses flying under the radar.

19. The T&E policy should be widely shared with all employees, including admins who might not travel but complete expense reimbursement reports for their bosses. This way everyone knows exactly what is expected.

20. When a receipt for expense reimbursement shows a weekend date, your processors should do a little research. Was the employee on a business trip? Is this employee one who is likely to entertain customers or suppliers on the weekend? A weekend expense deserves additional scrutiny. More than one employee has been known to entertain family and friends on the company dime. **DIYAP**

Receipts for Expense Reimbursement Documentation: Are You Collecting the Right Information

When it comes to receipts for documenting expense reimbursement requests, the devil certainly is in the details. Get it wrong and you could end up endangering your accountable plan status with the IRS – and that is something no organization wants to do. What's more, loose policies when it comes to receipts also make fraud just a little bit easier to commit. Take our quiz below to see how your policies stack up.

1. Do you require that your employees submit all receipts for expenditures $75 or more? ___ Yes ___ No

2. Do you require that your employees document meals and entertainment expenditures by including the names, titles and business relationships of all who attend a function (including meals)? ___ Yes ___ No

3. Do you require that one of your employees be present at all business entertainment functions? ___ Yes ___ No

4. Do you require that the highest level employee at a function pay for the function and submit the expense for reimbursement? ___ Yes ___ No

5. If an expense is for a meal, do you require the detailed meal receipt? ___ Yes ___ No

6. If your employee submits an expense reimbursement request that includes a hotel stay, do you require the hotel folio? ___ Yes ___ No

7. Does your travel and entertainment policy spell out in detail what is required when it comes to receipts? ___ Yes ___ No

8. Do you periodically run a report showing items submitted for reimbursement that are just below the receipt threshold? ___ Yes ___ No

9. If your employees scan receipts, do you periodically request to see the originals of a few receipts? ___ Yes ___ No

10. If an employee loses a receipt more than once in a rare while, do you require them to contact the business establishment and get a duplicate? ___ Yes ___ No

	Yes	No
Total	________	________

A Discussion of the Best Practice Responses

Clearly, the correct answer for all the questions was Yes. Let's see why.

1. The IRS requires documentation for all expenditures $75 or more. If you don't collect receipts to document expenditures, your accountable plan status could be in jeopardy.

2. The IRS also requires that you document meals and entertainment expenditures by including the names, titles and business relationships of all who attend a function (including meals). If your employees don't provide this information, your accountable

plan status could be in jeopardy.

3. The IRs also requires that one of your employees be present at all business entertainment functions.

4. This is not an IRS requirement but a sign of strong internal controls. No one should approve expenditures where they were a guest. By requiring the highest level employee at a function pay for the function and submit the expense for reimbursement you avoid this problem.

5. Requiring the detailed meal receipt is important for those organizations funded by grants. This is especially important if there is a no liquor clause. Not every organization asks for the detailed receipt and at this point it is not a recommended best practice. However, a growing number are starting to request it to ensure there are no extra guests or that the company isn't paying for unreasonable items.

6. Since meals are deductible from income taxes at a different rate than other expenses, it is necessary to identify meals separately. Normally this is not a problem unless an expense reimbursement request that includes a hotel stay. Then you should require the hotel folio, so the meal expenses can be broken out by the tax folks.

7. Avoid problems with travelers by spelling out in detail what is required when it comes to receipts used to document an expense reimbursement request.

8. By periodically running a report showing items submitted for reimbursement that are just below the receipt threshold, you can identify employees who might be abusing your expense reimbursement process. One or two requests shouldn't cause alarm, but a large number should raise a red flag and further investigation might be called for.

9. When your employees scan their own receipts, periodically request to see the originals of a few receipts. This will hopefully serve as a deterrent to those few employees who might be tempted to play games.

10. Everyone loses a receipt once in a while and one missing receipt is not likely to endanger your accountable plan status. However, if an employee loses a receipt more than once in a rare while or the dollar amount requested is large require the employee to contact the business establishment and get a duplicate. **DIYAP**

Best Practice Advice: Seeing T&E as a Regulatory Issue

When most people think about regulatory issues, travel and entertainment doesn't usually come to mind. But, truth be told, if your organization wants to deduct the expenses your employees spend on travel and entertainment for tax reporting purposes, you need to comply with a number of guidelines. And if per-diems are used, there are additional constraints. Let's take a look at these guidelines.

Deductible Expenses

Expenses are deductible if they are part of an "accountable plan." This is hugely important from a tax-reporting standpoint and can be used by those processing expense reports to ensure timely compliance.

To be included in the plan the following conditions must be met:

1) The expenses must have a business connection.
2) The employee must adequately account to the employer for these expenses within a reasonable period of time.
3) The employee must return any excess reimbursement or allowance within a reasonable period of time.

The 'Reasonable' Clause

If you've spent any time processing expense reports, the odds are high that what you consider reasonable and what the rogue employees in your organization do are not the same. Over time, the following timeframes have come to be considered appropriate with regards to the IRS definition of reasonable period of time.

Generally speaking:

- Employees must account for their expenses within 60 days of when the expenses were incurred.
- Employees must return any excess reimbursement (cash advances) within 120 days after the expense was paid or incurred.

The Per-Diem Rule

Some organizations, rather than covering actual living expenses for traveling employees, provide a fixed amount of money per day, to cover living and traveling expenses in connection with work. This is referred to as per-diems. Generally, employees either love per-diems or hate them. You can probably figure out which type of employee can make do on a per-diem and which type finds them restricting.

Effective January 1, 2007, employers who pay per-diems <u>in excess</u> of the federal rates have an additional concern if they do not:

- Track allowances;
- Require employees to substantiate expenses and turn back excess amounts; and
- Include the excess in the employees income.

Why? The entire amount of the expense allowance is subject to income and employment tax.

Per-Diem Rates

The GSA sets rate for the continental United States (CONUS). They are updated every October. You can find them by putting the words CONUS per diem in your search engine).

The Department of State sets rates for foreign travel. Information about those rates can be found at http://aoprals.state.gov/content.asp?content_id=184&menu_id=75

Mileage Reimbursement

The optional mileage reimbursement rate set by the IRS is 51 cents per mile for 2011. They key word here is optional. Not all organizations actually reimburse at the IRS rate with a small but measurable number reimbursing at a lower rate. Last year when *Accounts Payable Now & Tomorrow* surveyed its readers, none reported their organizations reimbursing at a rate higher than the optional IRS rate.

In recent years when gas prices skyrocketed within the year, the IRS issued an interim rate in the middle of the year. At least as we go to press, that does not seem likely to happen this year.

'Leverage' IRS Regs

Knowledge of the regulatory issues affecting travel and entertainment reimbursement helps organizations meet IRS tax reporting guidelines. It also provides a tool for middle-level managers to use for better expense reporting on the part of other employees within the organization. Let the IRS help you get those T&E laggards into shape! **DIYAP**

Best Practice Advice: Sample T&E Best Practice Guidelines

If there's one area in the corporate environment that's open to any and all sorts of misinterpretation it is travel and entertainment. Opinions on what's allowable and what's not can be all over the map.

1) **A well communicated T&E policy that is supported by top management.** This support has to be more than lip service, but real support. This means backing the processors should certain executives take liberties with their reimbursement requests as well as adhering to the policy themselves. The policy should be shared with everyone who travels as well as any admin staff who might prepare expense reports for their bosses.

2) **Easy access to T&E policy.** For most organizations this means posting it on the organization's Internet or Intranet site so any employee can check it should they have a question. This should not be a document with limited access

3) **Set rules and limits within the system.** By using automation to do some of the checking, policy violations are kept to a minimum and red flagged should they go through. This flagging can also be used to identify situations where preferred vendors were not utilized. While there are occasions when either not using a preferred vendor or not staying with the policy guidelines are allowable, the red flagging guarantees that there will be an investigation—and that alone is often adequate to deter some of your cowboys (and girls) from playing games.

4) **Insist on the use of a corporate T&E card and incorporate restrictions where appropriate.** Use of the corporate card puts an end to the games that a few employees play with their cards. This can include things like booking several flights and taking the cheapest while putting in for reimbursement for a more expensive one. It also allows for the aggregation of data to be used when negotiating with preferred vendors.

5) **Imaging of receipts.** By imaging all receipts you make it easy for approvers to view receipts before approving an expense report. It should be noted that some organizations are taking this review process one step further, requiring a check off in the system indicating they have looked at each receipt.

6) **Utilization of technology and upgrades.** For a long time, travel and entertainment expense reimbursement requests and reviews have been a heavily manual process. It still remains that way at many organizations. Stuart is a big proponent of taking advantage of technology to help with the process as well as all upgrades as they become available.

7**) Monitoring and multi-tiered approval process.** That's right multi-tiered approvals for expense reports over a certain dollar level. There's a double beauty for the tiered approval process. First, you get a second set of eyes reviewing larger expense reports. The second benefit relates to something we all know goes on in the business world. Many managers do not review expense reports before approving them. However, if they know the expense report will require a second approval—and in effect their work is being reviewed as well—they are more likely to take a close look at that expense report before putting their John Hancock on it.

8) **Consequences of violations.** Employees should know what the consequences of a policy violation are and they should also be made aware of what will happen if fraud is discovered on a reimbursement request. And, the company should enforce this stance across the board. This may seem harsh but if employees find they can steal a few dollars, in most cases they will ratchet up the fraud. **DIYAP**

Best Practice Advice: Some Simple Travel & Entertainment Best Practice Guidelines

If there's one area in the corporate environment that's open to any and all sorts of misinterpretation it is travel and entertainment. Opinions on what's allowable and what's not can be all over the map. This issue was just one of those discussed ata recent Accounts Payable Now & Tomorrow Webinar on T&E Fraud Prevention and Detection. Joining the discussion was Rohm and Haas Company's Craig Stuart. He is their North American Region manager of manufacturing services and travel. As part of the Webinar he identified some of the T&E best practices employed at Rohm and Haas. We thought they were well worth sharing with our readers.

1) **A well communicated T&E policy that is supported by top management.** This support has to be more than lip service, but real support. This means backing the processors should certain executives take liberties with their reimbursement requests as well as adhering to the policy themselves. The policy should be shared with everyone who travels as well as any admin staff who might prepare expense reports for their bosses.

2) **Easy access to T&E policy.** For most organizations this means posting it on the organization's Internet or Intranet site so any employee can check it should they have a question. This should not be a document with limited access

3) **Set rules and limits within the system.** By using automation to do some of the checking, policy violations are kept to a minimum and red flagged should they go through. This flagging can also be used to identify situations where preferred vendors were not utilized. While there are occasions when either not using a preferred vendor or not staying with the policy guidelines are allowable, the red flagging guarantees that there will be an investigation—and that alone is often adequate to deter some of your cowboys (and girls) from playing games.

4) **Insist on the use of a corporate T&E card and incorporate restrictions where appropriate.** Use of the corporate card puts an end to the games that a few employees play with their cards. This can include things like booking several flights and taking the cheapest while putting in for reimbursement for a more expensive one. It also allows for the aggregation of data to be used when negotiating with preferred vendors.

5) **Imaging of receipts.** By imaging all receipts you make it easy for approvers to view receipts before approving an expense report. It should be noted that some organizations are taking this review process one step further, requiring a check off in the system indicating they have looked at each receipt.

6) **Utilization of technology and upgrades.** For a long time, travel and entertainment expense reimbursement requests and reviews have been a heavily manual process. It still remains that way at many organizations. Stuart is a big proponent of taking advantage of technology to help with the process as welll as all upgrades as they become available.

7**) Monitoring and multi-tiered approval process.** That's right multi-tiered approvals for expense reports over a certain dollar level. There's a double beauty for the tiered approval process. First, you get a second set of eyes reviewing larger expense reports. The second benefit relates to something we all know goes on in the business world. Many managers do not review expense reports before approving them. However, if they know the expense report will require a second approval—and in effect their work is being reviewed as well—they are more likely to take a close look at that expense report before putting their John Hancock on it.

8) **Consequences of violations.** Employees should know what the consequences of a policy violation are and they should also be made aware of what will happen if fraud is discovered on a reimbursement request. And, the company should enforce this stance across the board. This may seem harsh but if employees find they can steal a few dollars, in most cases they will ratchet up the fraud.

By incorporating the practices Stuart enumerated into your organization's travel and entertainment expense program, you will strengthen it and limit your exposure to fraud. **DIYAP**

Regulatory

- The Regulatory Diagnostic
- The 1099 Diagnostic
- Unclaimed Property Best Practice Diagnostic
- Best Practice Advice: Unclaimed Property
- Best Practice Advice: Tax Information Reporting
- Best Practice Advice: The ABCs of Unclaimed Property Audits and Auditors: What You Need to Know

The Regulatory Diagnostic

Worker classification 1099s, expense reimbursement, and income paid to foreign vendors are all issues that are coming under increased scrutiny by the IRS. They are also areas often accounts payable is frequently responsible for. Use the checklist on page x to identify areas where you might have problems. The explanations on page x will explain the reasoning behind the correct response, the one that will keep you out of hot water with the IRS. It will also occasionally include more stringent recommended best practices. Apparently, AP Now is sometimes tougher than the IRS.

This diagnostic is a little different. Each item should be addressed from the standpoint of both Best Practices (BP) and IRS Requirements (IRS). Write Y (for Yes) or N (for No) for each in the space provided.

The Regulatory Diagnostic

1) Do you get a W-9 from every new vendor? Are you considering moving more of your smaller dollar purchases to p-cards to avoiding having to issue 1099s to certain smaller vendors in 2012? _____ BP ______ IRS
2) Do you classify workers as employees or independent contractors based on IRS criteria rather than management directives? _____ BP ______ IRS
3) Do your hire terminated or retired employees as consultants having them perform their old jobs while classifying them as independent contractors? _____ BP ______ IRS
4) Do you offer travelers cash advances? _____ BP ______ IRS
5) Do you have independent contractors performing the same work, under the same direction and conditions as employees? _____ BP ______ IRS
6) Do you require that all employees account for their expenses within 60 days of when the expenses were incurred? _____ BP ______ IRS
7) Do you require that all employees return any excess reimbursement (cash advances) within 120 days after the expense was paid or _____ BP ______ IRS
8) Do you keep track of which vendors supplied W-9s and which ones didn't? _____ BP ______ IRS
9) If you do not get W-9s but take the information verbally, do you keep track of who pro-

vided the information? _____ BP _____ IRS

10) If you did not get W-9s from every vendor in the past, have you begun collecting them? _____ BP _____ IRS

11) Do you use the IRS TIN Matching program? _____ BP _____ IRS

12) Do you run data from W-9s through the IRS TIN Matching program before you make the first payment to a new vendor? _____ BP _____ IRS

13) Are all the W-8s provided by your vendors original documents (not scanned or faxed)? _____ BP _____ IRS

14) Do you work all of your B-Notices? _____ BP _____ IRS

15) Do you protest all IRS fines and penalties no matter how small? _____ BP _____ IRS

16) Do you hold onto all documentation related to your IRS related issues, no matter how insignificant they may seem? _____ BP _____ IRS

17) incurred? _____ BP _____ IRS

18) If you pay per-diems in excess of the federal rates do you track allowances? _____ BP _____ IRS

19) If you pay per-diems in excess of the federal rates do you require employees to substantiate expenses and turn back excess amounts? _____ BP _____ IRS

20) If you pay per-diems in excess of the federal rates and do not require employees to turn in the excess over substantiated expenses, do you include the excess in the employees' income for tax reporting purposes? _____ BP _____ IRS

21) Do you take a refresher course once a year in 1099 issues? _____ BP _____ IRS

Explanation of the Diagnostic Responses

1. Do you get a W-9 from every new vendor? Recommended Best Practice: Yes; IRS Requirement: No. At this point in time the IRS does not require that you get W-9s, just the requisite tax identification information. However AP Now recommends you get the W-9 to avoid other problems. Most vendors have a W-9 readily available for their customers who ask.

2. Do you keep track of which vendors supplied W-9s and which ones didn't? Recommended Best Practice: Yes; IRS Requirement: No. However, without a tracking system, most organizations are going to be hard pressed to figure out which vendors they should solicit for TINs and which they already have on hand.

3. If you do not get W-9s but take the information verbally, do you keep track of who provided the information? Recommended Best Practice: Yes; IRS Requirement: No. Without knowing who provided a TIN, the company will have difficulty getting it corrected should it turn out there is a name/TIN mismatch.

4. If you did not get W-9s from every vendor in the past, have you begun collecting them? Recommended Best Practice: Yes; IRS Requirement: No. With corporate reporting just around the corner, the longer an organization waits to start collecting missing TIN information, the uglier the process will be.

5. Do you use the IRS TIN Matching program? Recommended Best Practice: Yes; IRS Requirement: No. The benefits of using TIN Matching include a huge reduction in B-Notices and a more efficient 1099 issuance process.

6. Do you run data from W-9s through the IRS TIN Matching program before you make the first payment to a new vendor? Recommended Best Practice: Yes; IRS Requirement: No. See explanation for #5.

7. Are all the W-8s provided by your vendors original documents (not scanned or faxed)? Recommended Best Practice: Yes; IRS Requirement: Yes.

8. Do you work all your B-Notices? Recommended Best Practice: Yes; IRS Requirement: Yes.

9. Do you protest all IRS fines and penalties no matter how small? Recommended Best Practice: Yes; IRS Requirement: Clearly No. If you just pay a fine (even if it is only a few hundred dollars) you are establishing a record of noncompliance. This will come back to haunt you at a later date should you try and protest a larger fine or penalty.

10. Do you hold onto all documentation related to your IRS related issues, no matter how insignificant they may seem? Recommended Best Practice: Yes; IRS Requirement: No. By having this documentation you will be able to demonstrate to the IRS that your intentions were in the right place, even if you were not 100% compliant with the law. This can go a long way should your organization be accused of willful disregard by the IRS.

11. Are you considering moving more of your smaller dollar purchases to p-cards to avoiding having to issue 1099s to certain smaller vendors in 2012? Recommended

Best Practice: Yes; IRS Requirement: No.

12. Do you classify workers as employees or independent contractors based on IRS criteria rather than management directives? Recommended Best Practice: Yes; IRS Requirement: Yes.

13. Do your hire terminated or retired employees as consultants having them perform their old jobs while classifying them as independent contractors? Recommended Best Practice: No; IRS Requirement: No.

14. Do you offer travelers cash advances? Recommended Best Practice: No; IRS Requirement: No. The IRS has no position on the offering of cash advances; only how they are accounted for.

15. Do you have independent contractors performing the same work, under the same direction and conditions as employees? Recommended Best Practice: No; IRS Requirement: No. Should you have a worker classification audit, the independent contractors would probably be reclassified.

16. Do you require that all employees account for their expenses within 60 days of when the expenses were incurred? Recommended Best Practice: No; IRS Requirement: Yes. While these guidelines are not in the IRS code, it is generally accepted that if you comply with these timelines, your Expense Reimbursement plan will maintain its "accountable" status. It is recommended that the accounting be done within 30 days. The IRS is lenient in this regard.

17. Do you require that all employees return any excess reimbursement (cash advances) within 120 days after the expense was paid or incurred? Recommended Best Practice: No; IRS Requirement: Yes. While these guidelines are not in the IRS code, it is generally accepted that if you comply with these timelines, your Expense Reimbursement plan will maintain its "accountable" status. It is recommended that the accounting be done within 45-60 days. The IRS is lenient in this regard.

18. If you pay per-diems in excess of the federal rates do you track allowances? Recommended Best Practice: Yes; IRS Requirement: Yes. Actually, if you use per-diems, the recommended best practice is to use the federal rates. It avoids a number of compliance and accounting issues.

19. If you pay per-diems in excess of the federal rates do you require employees to substantiate expenses and turn back excess amounts? Recommended Best Practice: Yes; IRS Requirement: Yes. Actually, if you use per-diems, the recommended best practice is to use the federal rates. It avoids a number of issues.

20. If you pay per-diems in excess of the federal rates and do not require employees to turn in the excess over substantiated expenses, do you include the excess in the employees' income for tax reporting purposes? Recommended Best Practice: Yes; IRS Requirement: Yes. Actually, if you use per-diems, the recommended best practice is to use the federal rates. It avoids a number issues.

21. Do you take a refresher course once a year in 1099 issues? Recommended Best Practice: Yes; IRS Requirement: No. Unbelievably, it seems that each year there are some changes in the guidelines for issuing 1099s. We expect the next few years to be a real challenge in this regard. The IRS offers no guidance on how professionals keep abreast of the changes each year. Professionals can take advantage of one

Are Your Procedures for Collecting TIN Information from Domestic Vendors up to Snuff?

Yes, it's okay to take taxpayer identification number information from your domestic vendors over the phone, but it's really not a good idea – and definitely not a best practice. As regulatory pressures increase, the collection of TINs for 1099 reporting purposes has gotten more important.

The checklist starts on the following page.

AP Now's 1099 Diagnostic Checklist

1. Do you get W-9s from all new vendors? ___ Yes ____ No

2. Have you signed up for the IRS TIN Matching Program? ___ Yes ____ No

3. Do you run all new vendor TIN information through TIN Matching? ___ Yes ____ No

4. Do you run this information through TIN Matching before making the first payment instead of waiting for the end of the year to perform this task? ___ Yes ____ No

5. Do you resolve all discrepancies reported by TIN Matching before making the first payment? ___ Yes ____ No

6. Do you track the receipt of all W-9s? ___ Yes ____ No

7. Do you follow up with those vendors who don't return W-9s? ___ Yes ____ No

8. Do you track the successful match in TIN Matching for each W-9? ___ Yes ____ No

9. Can you easily produce these records in case of an audit? ___ Yes ____ No

10. Do you have a written policy and procedures manual that addresses the collection of W -9s and the issuance of 1099s? ___ Yes ____ No

11. Do your practices mirror what is in your policy and procedures manual for both the collection of W-9s and the issuance of 1099s? ___ Yes ____ No

12. Do you keep up with all the changes in 1099 reporting requirements, getting the staff some education each fall? ___ Yes ____ No

13. Do you update your policy and procedures manual each year to reflect any regulatory changes? ___ Yes ____ No

14. Do your procedures assure you that the appropriate person receive the B-Notices as soon as your organization receives them, i.e. they don't sit on someone's desk in Tax for weeks before being sent to the appropriate staff for handling? ___ Yes ____ No

15. Do you immediately address B-Notices upon their receipt? ___ Yes ____ No

16. Is the handling of B-Notices addressed in your policy and procedures manual? ___ Yes ____ No

17. If you print your own 1099s, do you order your Forms early each year to ensure you have them in plenty of time? ___ Yes ____ No

18. Is your process set up to backup withhold, should that be necessary? ___ Yes ____ No

19. Have you considered going back and getting W-9s from existing vendors who you have not received W-9s from and don't issue 1099s to? ___ Yes ____ No

20. If you get a penalty notice, do you politely try to have it abated, even if it is a small dollar amount? ___ Yes ____ No

Total _____ Yes ____ No

Analysis of Correct Responses to the 1099 Diagnostic Checklist

Clearly, the correct response to all the questions was "Yes." You might want to review your procedures related to all your negative responses. Let's see why.

1. Getting a W-9s from all new vendors is the best way to ensure you collect the most accurate TIN information available. By getting it from every vendor and not just those you think you'll need to issue a 1099 for, you are preparing your organization for that inevitable day when we'll have to issue 1099s for corporates as well as independent contractors.

2. By signing up for the IRS TIN Matching Program you are taking the first step towards providing the IRS with the best information and minimizing the number of B-Notices you receive.

3. By running all new vendor TIN information through TIN Matching you are ensuring a match and minimizing the number of B-Notices.

4. Unfortunately some organizations sign up for TIN Matching and then use it once a year right before they issue their 1099s. Correcting mismatched information at this point can be a nightmare, especially if you are not doing business any longer with the vendor in question. Run the information through TIN Matching before making the first payment instead of waiting for the end of the year to perform this task puts you in the best position to correct mismatches easily.

5. Of course there's no good reason to sign up for TIN Matching and use it if you don't resolve all discrepancies reported by TIN Matching before making the first payment.

6. Some organizations send out requests for W-9s and then don't track the receipt of those returned. While this is better than doing nothing, it will leave you missing many W-9s.

7. Similarly, if you don't follow up with those vendors who don't return W-9s, you will not be in a good position to accurately issue all the 1099s you are obliged to issue.

8. Track the successful match in TIN Matching for each W-9 is critical to issuing correct, accurate 1099s each January.

9. Being able to produce your tracking records in case of an audit is critical to demonstrating good intent to the IRS. Otherwise, a lot of your efforts in this regards will not be rewarded.

10. A written policy and procedures manual that addresses the collection of W-9s and the issuance of 1099s is one way to ensure your processors are utilizing best practices with regard to your TIN collection efforts. It also helps new processors get started the right way.

11. Making sure your practices mirror what is in your policy and procedures manual for both the collection of W-9s and the issuance of 1099s is important. Otherwise your policy and procedures manual is meaningless.

12. It is critical that all organizations keep up with all the changes in 1099 reporting requirements, getting the staff some education each fall. The IRS is notorious for making changes every year. Why have all your efforts earn your organization a fine or penalty simply because you didn't make one small change. And, as everyone reading this is

probably aware, ignorance of the law is no excuse for not following it.

13. It is equally important that you update your policy and procedures manual each year to reflect any regulatory changes. Otherwise, should the IRS come in to audit, it will be difficult to demonstrate good intent and that you were handling matters correctly when your records say you weren't.

14. One of the numerous problems with B-Notices is sometimes getting them when they arrive at the company. The IRS will mail them to the person who signs the tax return. In most companies, this is not the same person who handles 1099s. In fact, in large companies, the person receiving the B-Notices will be many layers removed from the person dealing with them. Establish procedures that ensure the appropriate person receive the B-Notices as soon as your organization receives them.

15. Since you don't have a lot of time to address B-Notices, they should take top priority when they are received.

16. Many people forget to address the handling of B-Notices in their policy and procedures manual. Make sure your manual addresses the issue. This ensures that whoever is handling them knows what to do and it will demonstrate good intent to the IRS. As an added bonus, you'll have training material should someone new take over that position.

17. It would be a shame to do everything right and then not have the forms to print your 1099s. You'll end up paying rush shipping charges and there's really no need. If you print your own 1099s, order your Forms early each year to ensure you have them in plenty of time. Put it on your department's calendar for September first each year.

18. Sometimes, despite your best efforts, it will be necessary to backup withhold. Should that be necessary make sure your processes can handle that IRS requirement.

19. Consider going back and getting W-9s from existing vendors who you have not received W-9s from and don't issue 1099s to. Most tax experts believe the IRS will eventually be successful in getting corporate reporting put in place. Rather than wait, ask your active vendors for W-9s now. You can do this over a period of time, requesting the information from 20-100 vendors each week or month, whatever is appropriate for your business.

20. When many organizations receive penalties or fines from the IRS for small dollar amounts, they simply go ahead and pay them. They figure it's not worth their time or effort to get them abated. This is not a good idea. If you receive a penalty notice, politely try to have it abated, even if it is a small dollar amount. If you don't you are establishing a track record with the IRS – and not a good one. When you receive a large penalty and approach the IRS, they are less likely to be understanding given your "history" of noncompliance. That's how they will look at it. By paying the fines you are admitting guilt. So, regardless of the time and expense, try and get those small fines and penalties abated. Your future negotiations with the IRS are on the line. **DIYAP**

AP Now's Unclaimed Property Best Practice Diagnostic

1) Are you careful about which state you file your Unclaimed Property reports with? ___Yes ___ No

2) Do you follow up on all un-cashed checks 90 days after their issue date? ___Yes ___ No

3) Do you monitor changes in reporting dates and dormancy periods for all states where you are required to report? ___Yes ___ No

4) Do you separate un-cashed vendor checks from un-cashed payroll checks when reporting? ___Yes ___ No

5) Do you report your payroll separately from your vendor checks? ___Yes ___ No

6) Do you have a policy and procedures manual documenting your current procedures? ___Yes ___ No

7) Do your actual practices mirror what is in your procedures manual? ___Yes ___ No

8) Does someone regularly review and extinguish open receivers that should have been closed? ___Yes ___ No

9) Do they document and save the reasons they are closing the receivers? ___Yes ___ No

10) Do you document any checks you choose to reverse? ___Yes ___ No

11) Do you save the documentation related to all check reversals? ___Yes ___ No

12) Do you document why the reasons for voiding any checks? ___Yes ___ No

13) Do you save that documentation? ___Yes ___ No

14) Do you believe that if you don't have records going back as long as the state wishes to audit, you have no liability and they won't be able to require your organization to report and remit? ___Yes ___ No

15) Do you write off any un-cashed checks to miscellaneous income? ___Yes ___ No

Total Your Responses. We did not make a mistake with the labeling of Questions 14 and 15.

	Column A	Column B
Totals Questions 1-13	______ Yes	_____ No
Totals Questions 14-15	_____ No	______ Yes
Total	________	_________

An Explanation of the Best Practice Responses

Ideally, you have 15 in Column A and nothing for Column B. Let's take a look at the correct answers and why they are the right way to do things.

1. Care should be taken when selecting the state to file your Unclaimed Property reports with. Most will file with more than one state. If you file with the wrong state and the correct state audits, it will insist on being paid. You will be given no credit for the money filed incorrectly. What's more; you will have to approach the state where you filed incorrectly to get the refund yourself. That will take time, effort and a lot of documentation because the first state is not going to want to return the funds to you. Better to take a little extra time up-front determining the correct state.

2. Most states require that you do some due diligence before remitting. They do not want to get your money and have to immediately turn around and disburse it to the rightful owner. The states expect you to do that. Following up on all un-cashed checks 90 days after their issue date is considered adequate by the states. However, most experts suggest 60 days is a better alternative.

3. In their attempts to generate revenue, some of the states have been turning their attention do unclaimed property. By shortening dormancy periods they can improve revenues without increasing taxes. Monitoring this information is critical for accurate reporting. Similarly occasionally a state will change a reporting date.

4. Unfortunately, vendor checks and payroll checks typically have different dormancy periods. So it is important that you track un-cashed checks separately.

5. Likewise, you must report payroll separately from your vendor checks. More than an occasional company lumps payroll with vendor checks. This will get you in trouble on two counts. First, they are supposed to be reported separately and second, payroll checks typically have a shorter dormancy period than vendor checks. So, if payroll is lumped with vendor checks, you will be reporting and remitting far past the due date for payroll.

6. A policy and procedures manual documenting your current procedures is your first step towards demonstrating compliance with unclaimed property regulations. It is also the way you ensure best practices are implemented in your organization and that everyone who works on unclaimed property knows what they should be doing.

7. More than occasionally, an organizations policy and procedures manual delineates best practices but the organization doesn't follow them. Thus you need to take that second step. Not only do you need the manual, your employees performing the unclaimed property functions need to actually use them. You can make sure this happens by doing surprise audits.

8. In a few states, unclaimed property auditors have decided that open receivers represent unclaimed property. If they are successful, other states will follow. Regardless of what happens, leaving receivers open for more than a time period reasonable for your business is not a good practice. Someone should regularly review and extinguish open receivers that should have been closed.

9. Reviewing open receivers and extinguishing them if they shouldn't be open is the first step. But the reasons for the closing should be documented and saved to prove to audi-

tors that you had good reasons for closing the receivers.

10. Reversed checks also represent a gold mine for unclaimed property auditors. Document any checks you choose to reverse so you cannot be forced to report and remit them.

11. Make sure documentation related to all check reversals is saved. Otherwise, despite your best efforts, the auditors will claim those funds.

12. Voided checks represent a real issue because many don't handle the issue properly as far as unclaimed property auditors are concerned. Document you reasons for voiding any checks. This includes checks that are voided and reissued because the check was damaged at some point during the check production cycle.

13. As discussed above, save that documentation to avoid arguments with the auditors.

14. When a state does an unclaimed property audit, especially for the first time, it will get every last cent it is entitled to. Some believe that if they don't have records going back as long as the state wishes to audit, the state won't be able to require your organization to report and remit because of the lack of documents. This is patently not true. The state will estimate what you owe. And, this is the last thing you want happening. So, hold onto your records.

15. A few organizations write off un-cashed checks to miscellaneous income. This is not the correct process. One of the first things a competent auditor will do upon arriving to audit a company is to request the miscellaneous income account and documentation for what went in it. Un-cashed checks written off to miscellaneous income is a red flag for the auditor to stop and collect all the funds associated with that write-off. **DIYAP**

Best Practice Advice: Unclaimed Property

Without a doubt, every organization has to turn over unclaimed property to the states. But between the time the property becomes considered abandoned and you need to remit it to the state, there are ways to reduce your expense associated with this required divesture of funds. Tracey Reid, president of Reid Unclaimed Property explains how.

1) Invest the dormant unclaimed property that you are holding in an interest-bearing vehicle. As state laws require holders to safeguard unclaimed property for a significant period of time before turning it over to the states, your company has a significant opportunity to make some return on these funds while they are in legal limbo. Payroll checks that are dormant are to be held for a minimum of 1 year in most states, but other types of property, like accounts receivable credits and accounts payable checks are to be held for at least 3 years, if not 5 years, before they are turned over to a state as unclaimed property. Some states have 7 year holding periods for unclaimed amounts before they are reportable.

Industry averages show that checks are generally cashed within 90 days of their issuance, if they are ever going to be cashed at all. After credits or checks have aged 90 days and are still outstanding, chances are they will not be cashed or cleared until you do some extra follow-up. Once you have attempted to clear the issue up through the normal channels and the amounts appear to be un-resolvable, let them create some income to offset the cost to your company of maintaining the assets for the statutorily prescribed dormancy period.

Make the most of these funds by investing them while you are legally responsible to maintain the amounts. Even a short-term investment like a 6 month certificate of deposit will generally bear more interest than leaving the funds sitting in your company's checking account. Administering unclaimed property is a cost for companies. If you can recover something to off-set the cost of this burden, it would certainly help your bottom-line.

2) Implement service charges on dormant accounts. As a holder, you have the responsibility to maintain and safeguard funds in your possession that belong to someone else. This is the law. Obeying the law is costly. The states recognize that there is a financial cost that companies bear to maintaining outstanding unclaimed property. In order to offset the cost, most states allow companies to charge "reasonable" service charges on dormant accounts, as long as the holder follows strict guidelines.

The legal treatment of unclaimed property service charges and dormancy fees are not always limited to the unclaimed property laws in each state. Consumer protection laws, banking regulations, and other federal and state statutory provisions can affect these charges and you should have your legal advisor thoroughly review the entire body of law in this area for each state involved before you begin imposing any of these types of fees.

In states where dormancy fees and service charges are allowed to be applied to unclaimed property, there are generally criteria that must be met for the charges to be considered legitimate:

- An enforceable contract must exist between the Holder and the owner to establish the holder's right to impose the charge;
- The Holder must, in fact, regularly and consistently apply the charge without regularly refunding the charge if an owner claims the abandoned property; and
- The amount of the charge must be reasonable, based on the facts and circumstance of the transactions.

While some states, like Ohio, permit holders to deduct a small fee from the value of each unclaimed item remitted to cover their administrative costs, most states frown upon any attempt that Holders make to reduce the value of abandoned property for their own gain. Most Holders would be wise to avoid charging these types of service charges at all, but if you feel that you can legitimately meet the requirements, remember that they must be *strictly enforced*.

Your policy to apply service charges or dormancy fees must be clearly spelled out to your customer, in writing, somewhere conspicuous. Just putting notice of these charges in fine print somewhere in the transaction documents will most likely be disallowed as notice by unclaimed property enforcement agencies. You also have to be very consistent in both applying and not removing these service charges. If you regularly reinstate the service charges for people that complain, or good customers that come back after a period of being absent, you will fail to prove your case to an Unclaimed Property Administrator and the dormancy fees that you did not reimburse will be "reinstated" on your unclaimed property audit assessment.

You will also need to be reasonable about the rate and amount of any service charges that you impose. If the dollar or two a month that you charge after a gift certificate or savings account has been abandoned for the statutory dormancy period is to cover the cost of tracking the true owner, performing due diligence and paying for postage is reasonable, most administrators would probably allow the deductions. If, however, the amount of the charges is unreasonable, like $1 a day after the property reaches dormancy, and it appears that the sole purpose of the charges is to reduce the value of the outstanding unclaimed property to zero and avoid escheat, an administrator will probably disallow ALL of your dormancy charges. Service charges are tricky...these dormancy fees should carry a warning--"Proceed with Caution."

3) Reduce your administrative cost with early reporting. Unclaimed property laws require, generally, that you hold unclaimed property for the entire statutorily determined dormancy period before turning it over to the states in the hope that you, as the holder, will be better equipped to find the true owner than the state is. This is not always the case, however.

In many situations, your company has absolutely no way of contacting a true owner to return their funds. Maybe you have attempted to call or write them a letter and the number you have is disconnected and the letter was returned by the post office. You have reached a dead end. No matter how long you hold the unclaimed funds, chances are you are not going to be able to find the true owner. States understand this situation and will often permit holders to report funds early, with adequate explanation, IF A HOLDER ASKS PERMISSION.

I do not suggest that you just report all of your unclaimed property before the statutorily required dormancy period has passed. States will often just reject your filing and return the funds to you. You must contact the states that are due to receive the funds and request permission to file early, with appropriate reasons for doing so. If you do not wish to invest the unclaimed funds in an interest bearing vehicle to benefit your company, early reporting can free your company's personnel from the burden of administering dead-end unclaimed property a little early, thus saving you the costs of administering and protecting the assets.

CONCLUSION

Let's face it; administering unclaimed property costs your company time and man-power. This is a real financial burden. Over-filing because of accounting errors and allowing the dormant funds to sit without earning interest can cost a company real dollars that can otherwise be recovered. Even filing property early or implementing a modest dormant account service charge can reduce your company's cost of doing business. Lastly, once your unclaimed property compliance is running smoothly, don't forget to search for and recover any unclaimed funds in state coffers that rightfully belong to your company. The real price of unclaimed property administration is leaving your company's OWN money on the table.

Tracey Reid is president of Reid Unclaimed Property and author of *Unclaimed Property: A Reporting Process and Audit Survival Guide.* **DIYAP**

Best Practice Advice: Tax Information Reporting

This is the seventh in a series of short articles devoted to the basics of accounts payable*. They are intended for those new to accounts payable as well as those who'd like to review the basics. In this segment we provide an introduction to the Information Reporting requirements for any organization making payments to individuals. What follows is a look at the very basics of this topic. The brevity of this piece is not meant to suggest the information about this topic is limited. Nothing could be further from the truth.

What are Your Responsibilities?

According to the IRS, any person, including a corporation, partnership, individual, estate, and trust, who make reportable transactions during the calendar year must file information returns to report those transactions to the IRS. Persons required to file Information Returns to the IRS must also furnish statements to the recipients of the income. Filers who have 250 or more must file these returns electronically.

Transactions reportable on a 1099 are shown in the accompanying table. The most common items are highlighted, but all must be reported. The information must be sent to the recipient by January 31 and to the IRS by February 28.

The determination of who gets a 1099 is made on the basis of the recipients' classification. If the recipient is to get a 1099, then his or her tax payer identification number is required. For individuals this is the social security number. It is highly recommended that the IRS Form W-9 be used for this purpose, although at the current time this is not mandatory.

1099s and W-9s are for payments to US persons only. If a payment is made to a contractor who is a non resident alien, different rules and forms apply.

When 1099s Are Handled Incorrectly

The consequences of handling Tax Information Reporting requirements incorrectly can be quite severe. In addition to dealing with headache-inducing B Notices, six months to a year after the initial reporting, there can be penalties and fines for getting the information wrong. While there are limits on the amount of these fines, if a determination is made that the organization intentionally disregarded the rules, the limits no longer apply.

This is an area that has come under increased scrutiny and in all likelihood that inquiry from tax regulators and auditors will continue.

Best TIN Solicitation Practices

The following are not difficult to do, as long as everyone gets on board.

1) Get a W-9 from everyone you do business with before you make your first payment. Refuse to make the payment until a signed W-9 is received and verified.

2) Sign up for the IRS TIN Matching program and use it.

3) Verify the TIN information provided before making that first payment. If you get a mismatch, you can get corrected information while you still hold the trump card.

That's it: just three simple steps. By following these you will dramatically reduce the number of errors and B-Notices. And, there is one other factor. By following these steps you will be able to demonstrate to the IRS—should there be a problem—that you had in good faith done the due diligence required. This will go a long way towards having penalties and fines abated. **DIYAP**

Best Practice Advice: The ABCs of Unclaimed Property Audits and Auditors: What You Need to Know

"There has been a sharp increase in the number of unclaimed property audits in the last three years," says Tracey Reid, president of Reid Unclaimed Property. Reid should know; she represents companies going through audits often for the first time. She shared her considerable expertise at several recent Accounts Payable Now & Tomorrow events. Here's a look at what you can expect in terms of the auditors and the types of audits they conduct.

The Purpose of An Audit

Before discussing audit essentials it's important to understand the reasoning behind them. The purpose, says Reid, is to determine the true amount of unclaimed property in the possession of the holder for the period under audit.

What most people don't realize is there is no statute of limitations when it comes to unclaimed property. Audits can go back as long as 20 years, if this is your first audit. Once audited, you will not be re-audited (unless fraud is discovered) by the same state for the same period of time. However, an auditor from another state may show up on your doorstep. In fact, Reid points out, auditors talk to one another and if an auditor finds a lot of unreported property at your organization, he or she is likely to share that intelligence with auditors in other states.

Types of Auditors

There are basically two types of auditors: state auditors and contract auditors, sometimes referred to as third-party auditors.

The states have the authority to audit anyone who may have failed to report unclaimed property. They may send in their own employees or a third-party auditor. These are companies under contract with state (usually multiple states) who conduct audits on behalf of that state. They are compensated either by:

(1) A percentage of the unclaimed property they find; OR
(2) An hourly rate.

It is the former that causes all the trouble for those being audited. Contingency audits are prohibited in only a few states. Reid recommends that if you are being audited you request a state employee auditor, if that is possible.

The reason for the caveat possibility is some states do not have any auditors on salary and rely completely on third-party auditors.

Types of Audits

Unless you only do business in one state, purchase everything from vendors in that state, and all your employees live in the same state, your organization is likely to be subject to unclaimed property audits from more than one state. The types of audits are:

- Audits conducted by the states' unclaimed property division.
- Joint audits (conducted by a number of states).
- State authorized examination (SAE) conducted by a third-party audit company.

The third-party auditors are either paid by hourly rate or percentage of unclaimed property found. It should also be noted that most of the joint audits will be conducted by third-party auditors. In just about every instance you will end up with a better result if a state employee rather than a third party auditor does the audit. **DIYAP**

Management Issues: General

- Common Misconceptions that Get AP into Hot Water
- Electronic Accounts Payable Diagnostic
- The Worst Practice Checklist
- 12 Hiring Best Practice Checklist
- Best Practice Advice: Making Sure Your Organization Isn't Paying Someone It Shouldn't
- Best Practice Advice: Seven Often-Overlooked Practices that Make AP Less Efficient Than It Could Be

AP Now's Common Misconceptions that Get AP into Hot Water

Without a doubt, some professionals are lulled into a false sense of complacency by some old myths that have been around forever. These misconceptions can cause serious damage to your bottom line, if not handled correctly. The checklist below contains 20 such common views. See how many you think are true and how many false.

1. My employees would never steal from us. ___ True ____ False
2. The fact that my accounting system will not take duplicate invoice numbers protects us against duplicate payments. ___ True ____ False
3. Our vendors return all duplicate and erroneous payments immediately. ___ True ____ False
4. Since we have detailed instructions for our processors, we don't have to periodically check their work. ___ True ____ False
5. Our management would never pay for staff to attend a conference or seminar. ___ True ____ False
6. Electronic invoicing solutions are not for us. They are too expensive. ___ True ____ False
7. We issue some 1099s; probably not all that we should. This will be good enough for the IRS. ___ True ____ False
8. The best practice for un-cashed checks is to write them off against miscellaneous income. ___ True ____ False
9. Fraud is something that happens at other companies; it would never happen here, we're too big. No one would dare try and steal from us. ___ True ____ False
10. Fraud is something that happens at other companies; it would never happen here, we're too small. No crook would be interested in our activity. ___ True ____ False
11. We don't make electronic payments so we don't have to worry about these new frauds. ___ True ____ False

12. We use positive pay so we are completely protected against fraud.
___ True _____ False

13. Of course, management knows I'm interested in career advancement; I don't have to tell them. ___ True _____ False

14. Our employees have good common sense; we don't need a long detailed travel and entertainment policy to tell them what they shouldn't do. ___ True _____ False

15. A few of our managers allow their employees to take their spouses to dinner and expense it to the company. It doesn't really matter because it's only a few and no one will find out. ___ True _____ False

16. Our VP of Operations recently retired and is collecting his pension. He never really left; he continues doing the same job only now we pay him on a 1099 instead of a W-2. The IRS won't care because he's paying all the taxes. ___ True _____ False

17. Whenever a vendor doesn't charge us sales tax we simply add it to our payment. That way we don't have to mess with use tax and the states still get their money. Everyone should be happy. ___ True _____ False

18. We have an associate who processes invoices three times as fast as the others. She doesn't stick to our coding standard but we figure the few errors she might introduce are more than made up for by her speed. ___ True _____ False

19. Paying only from an original invoice will protect us completely against making a duplicate payment. ___ True _____ False

20. Keeping processors in the same position over the long haul is a good idea. They get to know the vendors' staff intimately can resolve discrepancies faster.
___ True _____ False

A Best Practice Discussion of the Reality behind the Theories

Clearly all the items in the above checklist are false. Now, let's see why.

1. Most employees would never steal from you. Unfortunately, a few would. Identifying those few bad apples is not easy. Hence strong internal controls and appropriate segregation of duties are always recommended in any accounts payable function.

2. The fact that my accounting system will not take duplicate invoice numbers protects you against duplicate payments only in theory. The reality is painfully different as processors find ways to "trick" the system into accepting the invoice a second time. Additionally, this control only works if the invoice number was entered correctly the first time. As more invoices are processed electronically, this control should work better.

3. The sad reality is that few vendors return any duplicate and erroneous payments at all. At 99% of all companies they become those infamous credits the accounts payable staff so diligently searches for.

4. While detailed instructions for your processors are a good starting point, that's all they are. If you don't periodically check their work short cuts potentially leading to inaccuracies will slip in on occasion.

5. Many professionals are stunned to find out that their management would pay for staff to attend a conference or seminar, if they only asked. Never assume you'll be turned down. Make a business case for attending showing how the company will benefit and see what happens.

6. Electronic invoicing solutions have come down tremendously in price. Some are available on a pay-as-you-go pricing scheme. If you haven't investigated e-invoicing in several years, you may be surprised at what you'll find.

7. Not surprisingly, the IRS expects every organization to issue every 1099 it is supposed to issue. Its reaction will not be pleasant if you are discovered to be slip shod in your issuance practices during an audit.

8. It is a worst practice to write un-cashed checks off against miscellaneous income. In fact, unclaimed property auditors will look at your miscellaneous income account as part of their audits knowing full-well that some companies are still using this awful practice.

9. Fraud doesn't discriminate. Being a large company just means there is more for the crooks to potentially get their hands on. It's up to you to make sure that doesn't happen..

10. Again, fraud doesn't discriminate. Crooks also know that sometimes smaller organizations have weaker controls. This makes these organizations a target as well.

11. The new frauds related to electronic payments have nothing to do with how you make payments and everything to do with your internal controls and how you treat your bank accounts.

12. Positive pay protects against most—but not all—check fraud; that is all. It does not protect against other types of fraud. While it is a recommended best practice that all organizations use positive pay, it is just the first step in any organization's fraud prevention and detection program.

13. It is a serious mistake to assume management knows you are interested in career advancement; you have to tell them. Too often it is assumed that a good employee is happy in his or her position so no one considers that person for a promotion. Make your wishes known in a professional manner. The annual review is a good time to share your wishes.

14. Most employees have good common sense; but unfortunately a few don't. That's why a long detailed travel and entertainment policy to tell them what they shouldn't do is a best practice.

15. There are more problems than you might imagine when a few even one manager allows employees to take their spouses to dinner and expense it to the company. For starters, this type of thing never stays secret. Word of it will spread like wildfire and the impact on employee morale is not good. But, that is the least of the problems. The IRS would not consider this a deductible expense as it does not meet its guidelines for an accountable plan. Also, if you were going to conform 100% with IRS guidelines, the employee in question should have the amount of the dinner included in his or her reportable income. A better approach would be to strictly prohibit this type of reimbursement in the company travel and entertainment policy.

1. The IRS is the one who sets the rules as to whether someone is an employee or an independent contractor. Companies that allow executives to retire (or outplace them) and then hire them back doing the same job paying them on a 1099 instead of a W-2 are courting big IRS trouble.

2. Vendors who don't charge sales tax typically don't do so because they also aren't required to do so. Usually, that is either because the item isn't taxable or they don't have nexus in the state in question. If they don't have nexus, they will not remit your money and you will still owe the use tax. Should you be audited, the state will expect you to pay the tax. Whether you are reimbursed by the vendor or not is not the state's concern.

3. One serious mistake will wipe out any savings you may have accrued thanks to an associate who processes invoices three times as fast as the others. It is imperative that everyone sticks to your coding standard.

4. Paying only from an original invoice used to be a great way to protect against making a duplicate payment. However, technology has made that approach meaningless. Today you can have many original-looking invoices and end up paying the same invoice numerous times if you rely on the 'only pay from an original' theory. Look for other ways to guard against duplicate invoices.

5. Keeping processors in the same position over the long haul does have some obvious benefits but it also has one overriding deficiency. This is why it in recommended that processors be rotated. When an associate works on an account for a long time, he or she will sometimes become friendly with the person handling the account for your supplier. This can be a good thing when there's a problem. But, it also makes collusion for fraud much more likely. That's why job rotation has become such a hot issue when it comes to fraud prevention. Job rotation is something any organization with more than one processor can do on a regular basis and is fast becoming a recommended best practice.. **DIYAP**

Your Electronic Accounts Payable Department Diagnostic

Most accounts payable departments, even those making significant inroads into the electronic world, are still overflowing with paper. This stark fact makes some of us feel like we're getting nowhere with the paperless revolution. The good news is we've come a whole lot farther than many realize. So, let's stop and do a departmental assessment to determine whether your accounts payable department should be classified as a dinosaur or a visionary. The following quiz will help you make that determination. Take the quiz, add up your score, and then check the box at the end to determine your classification

1) Using e-mail for communications (pick no more than one)

Use for over 25% or more, add 5 points.	____
Use for over 50%, add 10 points.	____
Use for over 75%, add 15 points.	____

2) Receive invoice electronically (pick no more than one)

Receive over 25% or more, add 5 points.	____
Receive over 50%, add 10 points.	____
Receive over 75%, add 15 points.	____

3) If you scan all paper invoices converting them to an electronic document, add 25 points. ____

4) Make as many payments as possible through the ACH or using p-cards. If you

Make over 25% of payments, add 10 points. _____
Make over 50%, add 15 points. _____
Make over 75%, add 20 points. _____

5) When making payments by check, if you use a bank to print and mail checks, add 10 points. _____

6) When making electronic payments, how do you send remittance information?
Don't send it, add zero points. _____
Send it by e-mail, add 10 points. _____
Send it by snail mail, subtract 10 points. _____

7) If you get approvals on invoices using workflow or e-mail, add 20 points. _____

8) If everyone within the organization has online access to review invoice and check status, add 10 points. _____

9) If you use an online dispute resolution model to resolve discrepancies with vendors, add 15 points. _____

10) If vendors can check the status of their invoices and payments online, add, 20 points. _____

11) For T&E reimbursement
If 100% are via ACH, add 20 points _____
If checks are used and mailed home 100% of the time, add 10 _____
If checks are printed and employees allowed to pick them up, subtract 20 points _____

Total _____

Dinosaur or Visionary?

So, how'd you do? While we hope you had a little fun taking our quiz, the real goal is to help readers identify those areas where they can make some process improvements to take advantage of the "Electronic Accounts Payable Office." It also identifies those practices that are a serious drain on departmental efficiency—and we don't have to tell you what to do with them!

The AP Dinosaur or Visionary Scorecard

Score	Classification
< 25	AP Dinosaur, definite room for improvement.
26-50	AP Apprentice, you've taken the first steps, keep going.
51-75	AP Steady Eddie/Edith, you're on the right track, just a few changes could make a *big* difference.
76-100	AP Geek, a few more tweaks and you'll be in Superstar territory.
101- 125	AP Superstar, pretty impressive; well on your way to visionary status.
Over 125	AP Visionary—WOW!!! **DIYAP**

Eliminating Worst Practices in Accounts Payable

There's always a good deal of discussion about best practices in accounts payable. But rarely do we focus on the reverse. AP Now believes it is important to identify those practices that are detrimental to the running of an efficient, fraud-resistant function. The quiz on page 8 will help you determine if you are employing any of these productivity busters in your own operation.

The Worst Practice Checklist

1) Does your organization get W-9s only from vendors they think they will have to issue 1099s to? ___ Yes ___ No

2) Does your organization take Taxpayer Identification information over the phone? ___ Yes ___ No

3) Does your organization run all its TIN information through TIN Matching at one time at the end of the year? ___ Yes ___ No

4) Does your organization limit its contact information to the Remit-To address? ___ Yes ___ No

5) Does your organization update your contact information only when the vendor informs you of a change? ___ Yes ___ No

6) Does your organization allow the return of check to requisitioners as a matter of practice? ___ Yes ___ No

7) Does your organization have a petty cash box? ___ Yes ___ No

8) Does your organization allow Rush checks? ___ Yes ___ No

9) Does your organization let vendors email invoices to whomever they feel appropriate? ___ Yes ___ No

10) Does your organization share a fax machine to receive invoices with other departments? ___ Yes ___ No

11) Does your organization give cash advances to all travelers? ___ Yes ___ No

12) Are any of your employees able to access and make changes to your complete accounting system? ___ Yes ___ No

13) Does your organization leave p-cards and T&E cards with departing employees? ___ Yes ___ No

14) Has your organization failed to review and update its accounts payable policy and procedures at least once a year? ___ Yes ___ No

15) Has your organization eliminated funds in its budget for employee training? ___ Yes ___ No

Total _____Yes _______No

A Discussion of the Worst Practices Checklist

Clearly, or at least we hope it is apparent, the best answer to each of these questions is No. IF you scored a total of 15 in the no column you deserve a round of applause. Every Yes indicates the use of one less-than-ideal practice. Let's see why each of these practices should be eliminated.

1. Getting W-9s only from vendors they think they will have to issue 1099s to puts you at risk for not issuing all the 1099s you will be required to issue. What's more, if at some point in the future the IRS decides to require 1099s for everyone (as many expect) you will have a monumental task on your hands trying to collect all the missing information. Better to start now and kill two proverbial birds with one stone.

2. Taking Taxpayer Identification information over the phone, while currently acceptable to the IRS, puts you at risk for numerous errors. Your employee could incorrectly write down a number or the vendor could supply the wrong one. You will never know until one of those awful B-Notices shows up. Avoid all these potential problems by requiring a W-9 instead of taking the information verbally.

3. While running all TIN information through TIN Matching at one time at the end of the year may seem like a time saver, it is anything but that. When a mismatch is found, it is relatively easy to get it corrected if you have not paid the vendor. However, if the vendor has been paid and/or you are no longer doing business with that entity, there is no reason for them to cooperate. By waiting it will be more difficult for you to locate the right person at the vendor to fix the information.

4. Limiting the contact information to the Remit-To address creates problems when you need to contact the vendor to check out something or mail them some communication about a change in policy. Since many Remit-To addresses are bank lockboxes, it will be difficult to get in touch with the vendor using the information in your master vendor file if you only have the Remit-To address.

5. Updating contact information only when the vendor informs you of a change will quickly result in dirty contact data in your master vendor file. Actively update it yourself periodically or contract with an outside firm to do it for you.

6. Returning checks to requisitioners as a matter of practice demonstrates poor internal controls and in more than a few instances has facilitated employee fraud. Most organizations forbid this practice or if it is allowed require a form to be filled out and approved by a senior manager.

7. Petty cash boxes create more problems than they solve. Given the wide acceptance of credit cards, the need for petty cash boxes has been almost completely eliminated. There are other ways to reimburse employees for cash expenditures and they should be utilized.

8. Allowing more than the occasional Rush check is a sign that the accounts payable function isn't work as it should. Review your processes to see where they can be improved. Examine the causes for the emergency checks and fix the problems that you find. All Rush payments should be made via the ACH. Issuing a check for emergency payments creates additional problems.

9. Letting vendors email invoices is a good idea however the invoices should be sent to one central email address for processing. If they are sent to numerous locations there

is no guarantee they will end up in the right place on a timely basis for processing. Rewrite your procedures to incorporate the centralized email address for the receipt of invoices.

10. Accepting invoices via fax has gone from being a worst practice to a best practice. However for this to work effectively, accounts payable should have a separate fax machine for this purpose. Share the fax machine where invoices are received with other departments is almost a guarantee that someone will inadvertently pick up an invoice and lose it.

11. Giving cash advances to all travelers is no longer a requirement. Airfare, hotels, meals, car rentals, most incidentals and many taxi rides can now be charged. This obviates the need for cash advances. What's more; cash advances tend to create other problems in the reimbursement process. Eliminating them is considered a best practice.

12. If even one of your employees is able to access and make changes to your complete accounting system your segregation of duties regime is in jeopardy. No one, no matter what their level in the organization, should have access to everything.

13. Not retrieving p-cards and T&E cards from departing employees is a small but potentially costly mistake. Whether the employee was terminated by the organization or left to take a fabulous new job, the card should be retrieved as part of the exit interview process just as the employee identification card and any keys to the building or office are returned. If the card is left with the employee there is the potential for unauthorized charges. Additionally, the cards should be cancelled with the card issuer.

14. By failing to review and update its accounts payable policy and procedures at least once a year you are almost guaranteeing the policy will be out of date. If it goes more than a few years without an update, it will not be worth the paper it's printed on and it definitely will not be able to be used as a training tool.

15. Unfortunately, quite a few organizations eliminated funds their budgets for employee training. This is being penny wise pound foolish, to quote an old proverb. A few dollars spent towards making sure employees are kept up to date will minimize fraud risk, ensure regulatory compliance as well as keep your processes up-to-date taking advantage of the latest innovations. These help with both efficiency and cost reductions.

So how did you stack up? Have you identified a few places where you need to revise processes so you can eliminate weak ones which could cause problems at some point? Or, were you one of the lucky few with either no issues or perhaps only one? **DIYAP**

Are Your Hiring Skills Up to Snuff?

Inevitably, no matter how good a manager you are, you will have to fill an open position. Typically, it is because someone has left. They have either procured a job in another company or department, retired or perhaps were invited to leave. Of course, if you are really lucky, your company is expanding so quickly, you have to expand staff in accounts payable. Now that you've got to hire someone, are you certain you're using the best practices to ensure you'll end up with the candidate who is the best fit? Use our Hiring Best Practice Checklist below to make that determination.

1. Do you create a detailed targeted job description and advertisement for the position you wish to fill? ___ Yes ___ No
2. Do you post the advertisement not only on your organization's website, but in a variety of other places where professionals interested in the position might see it? ___ Yes ___ No
3. Do you let all your networking contacts know you have an open position so they can refer anyone in their network who might be a good fit? ___ Yes ___ No
4. Do you prepare a targeted list of questions to ask each candidate before you start your interviews? ___ Yes ___ No
5. When selling the position and the company, do you share the negatives as well as the positives? ___ Yes ___ No
6. Do you review the candidates resume before they arrive so you don't waste valuable interview time asking questions when you can read to get the information much more quickly? ___ Yes ___ No
7. Do you ask open-ended questions rather than questions that require a simple Yes or No answer? ___ Yes ___ No
8. Have you created several typical but difficult scenarios ahead of time to ask the candidate about how they would handle the situation? ___ Yes ___ No
9. Do you ask the candidate for best practice recommendations to determine if he or she keeps current in the field? ___ Yes ___ No
10. Do you give the candidate time to ask questions? ___ Yes ___ No
11. Do you take notes during the interview? ___ Yes ___ No
12. Do you have one or two members of your staff interview the final candidates? ___ Yes ___ No
13. Do you allow these interviews to take place without monitoring them – so both the candidate and your staffers will feel free to say what they really think? ___ Yes ___ No
14. Do you let the staffers who've interviewed job candidates weigh in with their opinion before you make the final hiring decision? ___ Yes ___ No

15. Do you make some notes about the candidate as soon as the interview is over?
___ Yes ___ No

16. Do you fully consider team dynamics and how this person will fit in before making the final decision? ___ Yes ___ No

17. Have you posted the job internally? ___ Yes ___ No

18. Do you differentiate between skills a candidate must have and those you can teach when evaluating candidates? ___ Yes ___ No

19. Do you make the final selection based on who will fit in best and do the best job rather than who you liked best? ___ Yes ___ No

20. Do you notify candidates who were not selected of this in a timely manner?
___ Yes ___ No

A Discussion of the Best Practice Responses to the Hiring Best Practice Checklist

Once again, the ideal responses should be positive. Let's take a look at why.

1. By creating a detailed targeted job description and advertisement for the position you wish to fill, you ensure candidates with needed skills apply and those without them don't. If you don't delineate required skills, you'll waste time reviewing resumes and interviewing candidates who you simply won't be able to hire.

2. If you post the advertisement only on your organization's website, the number of people who see it will be limited. If, on the other hand, you post it in a variety of other places where professionals interested in the position might see it, you'll widen possible pool of candidates to select the best prospect from.

3. Similarly, by letting all your networking contacts know you have an open position, they can refer anyone in their network who might be a good fit, further widening the pool of qualified candidates.

4. By preparing a targeted list of questions to ask each candidate before you start your interviews, you'll ensure you ask everyone for the same information. There's nothing more frustrating than realizing after the fact that you forgot to ask a key question of some of your candidates. This is not to say that if a good question occurs to you once you've started interviewing, you shouldn't use it. You most definitely should add it to your list.

5. When selling the position and the company, share the negatives as well as the positives. While it might be tempting to gloss over the negatives, it is not fair to the candidate nor are you doing yourself any favors. While you might hire your first choice by not sharing an unpleasant aspect of the job, that person is likely to be out the door at the first opportunity and you'll be back looking to fill the position in relatively short order. What's more, you want to start the relationship off on a good foot, and that is not apt to happen if the new hire realizes they were not given an accurate picture during the interview.

6. Review the candidates resume before they arrive so you don't waste valuable interview time asking questions when you can read to get the information much more quickly. Spend valuable interview time getting to know the candidate and getting the information you need to determine if they can really do the job and if they will be a good fit with the rest of

your team.

7. By asking open-ended questions rather than questions that require a simple Yes or No answer, you'll be able to better size up the candidate. If you listen carefully, you'll see how they think and how they present themselves.

8. By creating several typical but difficult scenarios ahead of time to ask the candidate about how they would handle the situation, you'll get an idea of how they think and act under pressure. If you ask the same question of all candidates you'll be able to accurately compare how they would react when faced with a thorny dilemma.

9. By asking candidates for best practice recommendations you'll be able to determine if he or she keeps current in the field. It will give you an idea of whether or not that person will be able to make good process improvement suggestions as new technologies and practices are introduced.

10. Not giving the candidate adequate time to ask questions is a sign of a poor interviewer. The questions the candidate asks will also tell you something about them. Someone who immediately inquires about sick time policy demonstrates a different career commitment than someone who asks about your processes or if you have ever considered using a particular best practice. Of course, some candidates won't have any questions.

11. When interviewing a series of candidates, it is not a good idea to rely on your memory to remember their answers. Take notes during the interview to insure you have all the information available when making your final hiring decision.

12. If you are hiring someone to work with your team, it is critical that person get along well with your other employees. By having one or two members of your staff interview the final candidates, you'll get an idea as to who will fit in best.

13. While it is tempting to listen in when your staff is interviewing potential candidates, resist the temptation. This will allow both the candidate and your staffers will feel free to say what they really think. Occasionally, you'll have a candidate who is excellent at managing up but is an awful team player. This will become readily apparent to your staff, if they interview without you.

14. After your staffers have interviewed job candidates, let them weigh in with their opinion before you make the final hiring decision. If they have some concerns about your top choice listen carefully to determine if they are valid.

15. Don't rely on your memory. Make some notes about the candidate as soon as the interview is over. Otherwise, there's a reasonable chance you won't remember which candidate said what – and will end up hiring the person you "liked" best and not necessarily the best person for the job.

16. Don't underestimate the importance of team dynamics and how this person will fit in before making the final decision. This is critical when you are hiring for a position that requires a lot of interaction with other members of your staff.

17. Don't forget to post the job internally giving current employees the opportunity to apply for the position. Often there will be someone on staff who it would never occur to you to offer the job to who wants it – and who will do a good job for you. Best of all, they don't have to be taught about the company, you know how they perform and they understand the corporate culture and unwritten hierarchies in the organization.

18. By differentiating between skills a candidate must have and those you can teach when evaluating candidates, you'll end up with the person who fits in your group best. You won't have eliminated perfectly good candidates who might be missing one skill you consider essential – but really isn't. When deciding which skills are absolutely necessary, consider whether you could teach the missing attribute to an otherwise perfect candidate in relatively short time.

19. Occasionally we are swayed by a personable candidate whose primary skill might be making people like them. They turn out to be a disaster when it comes to doing the everyday work. Make the final selection based on who will fit in best and do the best job rather than who you liked best.

20. Don't forget the last and probably least pleasant step of the hiring process. Notify candidates who were not selected for the position in a timely and polite manner. Let them down as gently as you can. Too many times, this last step is not completed – and that is just not fair. **DIYAP**

Best Practice Advice: Making Sure Your Organization Isn't Paying Someone It Shouldn't

On top of all the other checks an accounts payable department has to do in order to make sure they are making an accurate payment, there are three that are often overlooked. It is imperative that your organization not pay terrorists, narcotics traffickers or dead people. Now, before you think we've lost our mind, please read on. Falling into one of these traps is easier than you might imagine. And, if you do, the consequences can be extremely painful financially.

Terrorists

Many reading this are probably thinking they would recognize a terrorist if they saw one and besides that their organization doesn't do business with anyone even closely resembling one. Don't be lulled into a false sense of security. A smart terrorist—and most of them are quite bright—will masquerade as a regular business. The first time I did research on this topic, I reviewed the OFAC list closely. There are companies on the list with innocuous sounding names like "The Bamboo Company."

The Office of Foreign Assets Control (OFAC) of the US Department of the Treasury administers and enforces economic and trade sanctions based on US foreign policy and national security goals against targeted foreign countries and regimes, terrorists, international narcotics traffickers, those engaged in activities related to the proliferation of weapons of mass destruction, and other threats to the national security, foreign policy or economy of the United States. You'll sometimes hear the list of terrorist organizations you shouldn't pay referred to as the OFAC list.

Drug Traffickers

The terrorists are included on a list called Specially Designated Nationals List (SDN). As part of its enforcement efforts, OFAC publishes a list of individuals and companies owned or controlled by, or acting for or on behalf of, targeted countries. It also lists individuals, groups, and enemies, such as terrorists and narcotics traffickers designated under programs that are not country specific. Collectively, such individuals and companies are called "Specially Designated Nationals" or "SDNs."

Not only are their assets blocked, U.S. persons are generally prohibited from dealing with them. The fines for violations can be substantial. Criminal and/or civil penalties can be levied. In extreme cases, jail time may be called for. Depending on the program, criminal penalties can include fines ranging from $50,000 to $10,000,000 and imprisonment ranging from 10 to 30 years for willful violations. On the civil side, penalties range from $250,000 or twice the amount of each underlying transaction

When it comes to identifying terrorists or terrorist organizations, there is no such thing as an eyeball test. Savvy terrorists once identified simply change their organization and come calling again wearing a new name.

What You Must Do
Before any payments are made, your potential payees should be run against the latest SDN list. It can be found at

http://www.treasury.gov/resource-center/sanctions/SDN-List/Pages/default.aspx

Many organizations routinely check new vendors against the SDN list when they set them up. Doing this is a good idea but it does not mean that you are good forever. The SDN list is updated regularly and payees should be checked against it each time a payment is made. Many organizations take a short cut of only getting the updates and running them against their master vendor file once a month. While this is definitely a good practice, you still run the risk of having someone slip through in the interim.

Dead People

Here's another example of a check you probably should do that may seem ludicrous at first but upon closer examination makes sense. This is especially important for those making one-time payment to individuals or vendors they are unlikely to do business with again. It is especially important for casinos.

Let's focus on the casino example because it is the easiest to understand. Someone goes to a casino and has a big win. The casino is required to issue a 1099. Now, if the person in question has been through this routine, they may just provide an incorrect social security number. After they got burned a few times, the casinos started using the IRS TIN Matching. Now, this will catch most mistakes but not all.

Savvy gamblers know that TIN Matching only checks the first four or five letters of the name. So, more than a few have found that by using someone else's social security number whose name is close to theirs, they can get around this stumbling block. A dead person's number is ideal because no one gets dinged. So, casinos routinely check not only using TIN Matching but also the Death Master File (DMF). Information about this file can be found at http://www.ssdmf.com/FolderID/1/SessionID/%7BA18FA896-9FA3-49D8-BE79-1455ACEB77B1%7D/PageVars/Library/InfoManage/Guide.htm

While not all situations call for a check of the DMF, more than a few will. If you are paying one-time vendors, especially if they are individuals, a check of the DMF might be something you should add to your routine.

Closing Thoughts

There are many issues to consider when making payments in accounts payable. Not only do you have to include routines to make sure your payments are accurate and not being made twice, you also need to take steps to ensure payments are being made to the right party. Concerns about breaking the law are also critical even when it seems completely unlikely. These issues are just one more example of how it is imperative that accounts payable professionals stay on top of their game. **DIYAP**

Best Practice Advice: Seven Often-Overlooked Practices that Make AP Less Efficient Than It Could Be

You've heard the old adage, work smarter not harder. Sometimes we've been doing things a certain way for so long in accounts payable, it never occurs to us to try another approach. That's where the smarter issue comes in. Sure, it's possible to improve productivity if you spend a lot of money, but that's not what we're talking about. Let's take a look at five practices that would make any accounts payable function run a little more efficiently—and won't require special budget allocations to do so.

1) Start accepting invoices both by e-mail and fax. For many years, companies refused to do this because they were concerned about duplicate payments. But now, we know that it is possible to have originally looking documents that are actually copies so not paying from a copy does not provide the protection it once did. By accepting invoices by email and fax you speed up the mail time making it easier to earn early payment discounts. What's more, if you are scanning invoices, an emailed invoice removes the need to scan.

2) Get rid of petty cash boxes, if you still have them. Anecdotal evidence suggests that approximately one-quarter of all organizations still have petty cash boxes. They are huge time wasters, are rarely in balance, and may tempt employees with financial issues. By eliminating petty cash boxes you will make the accounts payable function more efficient and you'll strengthen internal controls. And as an added benefit, your staff will probably be thrilled not having to deal with the sometimes questionable reimbursement requests.

3) Return invoices addressed inappropriately/addressed to no one to the vendor with a polite letter explaining that in order to process invoices efficiently it is imperative that every invoice contain the name of the requisitioner or a purchase order number. Without one of these vital pieces of information, your staff will waste time trying to figure out who ordered the item. You'll also eliminate those fraudulent invoices sent by crooks hoping to entice you to pay.

4) Develop and use strong coding standards for invoices and data entry in the master vendor file. Put it in writing and insist everyone use it. This simple approach will eliminate a good portion of potential duplicate payments. Don't assume everyone would use the same abbreviations as you would. They won't. And, by putting it in writing and giving a copy to every processor, they can refer to it if they have any questions.

5) Eliminate as many paper checks as you can. This can be done by moving small dollar items to p-cards and trying to pay as many vendors as possible using ACH. Paper checks are incredibly inefficient; they require a lot of manual handling, get lost in the mail and are expensive, to boot. On the other hand, electronic payments require no manual handling, are less expensive than paper checks and have very few or no unclaimed property issues.

6) Don't play favorites with employees from other departments (or for that matter from your own). Don't make exceptions against policy based on how much you like a person. For example, if you always do Rush checks for Jane in accounting, other employees will expect similar treatment. If you don't extend them the same courtesy there's bound to be a lot of complaining and grumbling and accounts payable's image will take a hit. What's more, eventually other groups will figure out who your favorites are and those

people will be recruited to come down and ask for exceptions for the rest of their department. Often, when accounts payable plays favorites, it is thought that no one knows. But, like all other gossip in an organization, it spreads faster than anyone might imagine.

7) Don't entertain special requests from vendors to pay them faster than the payment terms agreed to in their contracts. More than occasionally, a vendor will call and ask/demand to be paid more quickly than agree upon terms. Sometimes they'll claim someone in purchasing promised this. Other times, especially when they have gotten to know the processor handling their account well, they'll simply ask for a special favor trying to convince the processor to enter an early due date. While you want your processors to have good relations with your vendors, these relations need to be arm's length and not result in inappropriate actions. This is the first step down that slippery path of fraud due to collusion. While a processor putting something in for payment earlier than it should be paid is not a guarantee that fraud will occur in the future, it is a poor practice and should not be tolerated. Preventing this type of familiarity is another reason for regularly rotating processors.

As you can see, none of the above recommendations require budget allocations. All can be implemented without spending any money. Okay, the not accepting invoices without the name of the requisitioner or a purchase order number does require a postage stamp and an envelope. But you can use a form letter and you don't need budget approval for postage stamps.

These are just a few examples of strategies any organization can implement in their accounts payable department to make it a little more efficient. And, we're certain, if you put your mind to it, you can identify a handful of other practices that will improve departmental productivity without incurring a huge expense. **DIYAP**

Management Issues: Control

- Fraud Deterrence/Prevention/Detection Diagnostic
- Internal Control Best Practice Diagnostic
- Productivity Killer Checklist
- Best Practice Advice: Looking for Fraud in All the Right Places
- Best Practice Advice: Segregation of Duties: How Much Access Do Your Employees Really Have?
- Best Practice Advice: 5 Ways to Protect Your Organization From Payment Fraud

The Fraud Deterrence/Prevention/Detection Diagnostic

Internal controls have always played a strong role in preventing fraud but it's only recently that they've begun to get the attention and respect they deserve. In fact, it took some of the largest frauds in history (Enron, etc.) to finally get the business community to focus on internal controls. And now, with what's been going on in the financial markets, *Accounts Payable Now & Tomorrow* is concerned that the focus might not have been intense enough. That's why we have prepared this diagnostic for our readers to use to identify weakness in your process—potential land mines that could open your organization up to internal fraud.

1) Do you expressly forbid employees from sharing passwords? ___ Yes ___ No

2) Do your require employees to change passwords to access your system periodically, say every three to six months? ___ Yes ___ No

3) Do you require all employees who have anything to do with the payment process to take at least five consecutive days of vacation? ___ Yes ___ No

4) Do you prohibit the ability to both approve invoices and enter invoice data? ___ Yes ___ No

5) Do you prevent one or more of your managers/executives from having access to all phases of the payment process, even though it might make training and managing more difficult? ___ Yes ___ No

6) Do you have a strong policy prohibiting the return of checks to requisitioners? ___ Yes ___ No

7) Are all changes made to the master vendor file periodically checked? ___ Yes ___ No

8) Do you periodically (at least once a year) deactivate inactive accounts in your master vendor file? ___ Yes ___ No

9) Do you have an anonymous tip hotline? ___ Yes ___ No

10) Do you periodically check that your processors are not writing their passwords down where anyone can see them? ___ Yes ___ No

11) If you have a petty cash box, do you make sure that the location of the key is not common knowledge? ___ Yes ___ No

12) Do you wait until the end of the day to deliver checks to the mailroom for mailing? ___ Yes ___ No

13) Are unsigned checks always left in a secure location while waiting for signature – and not on someone's desk in an empty office? ___ Yes ___ No

14) Is the positive pay file uploaded only when checks are mailed? ___ Yes ___ No

15) Are checks only printed when they are going to be mailed—not earlier so they will reflect a date that matches your payment terms? ___ Yes ___ No

16) Are open receivers and POs always extinguished when an invoice is paid even if the invoice is paid outside accounts payable? ___ Yes ___ No

17) Is access to the master vendor file for entering vendors or changing vendor information severely limited? ___ Yes ___ No

18) When an employee making electronic payment transfers is terminated or leaves voluntarily, is the bank immediately notified and passwords changed? ___ Yes ___ No

19) When an employee is terminated or leaves voluntarily is the p-card administrator immediately notified so the p-card can be cancelled? ___ Yes ___ No

20) When a new vendor is to be entered into the master vendor file, do you require at least two signatures or approvals before adding? ___ Yes ___ No

21) When a new vendor is to be entered into the master vendor file, do you do some checking to make sure the vendor is legitimate before adding? ___ Yes ___ No

22) Are your approving managers held personally responsible if they approve a travel & entertainment expense report with obvious fraud? ___ Yes ___ No

23) When multiple employees attend the same function or restaurant meal, do you require the highest-level person to pay and submit the expense for reimbursement? ___ Yes ___ No

24) If you have a petty cash box, do you hold surprise audits and does everyone know you do that? ___ Yes ___ No

25) Do you have a written fraud policy, signed by a top-level executive, indicating zero tolerance for employee fraud? ___ Yes ___ No

Explanation of the Diagnostic Responses

The preferred response, as most readers have probably concluded, to all the questions is yes. A negative response does not indicate fraud but rather that the controls surrounding that issue are weak and your organization is vulnerable. Nearly every organization will have at least a few areas that are less than perfect when it comes to internal controls. Look into them and determine if it is possible to tighten the controls or if you have to live with the weaker controls. If you cannot implement the best practices suggested here, regularly audit your problem areas. **DIYAP**

The AP Now Internal Control Best Practice Diagnostic

Weak internal controls lead to a myriad of problems starting with duplicate payments and opening the door to fraud. They also translate into an inefficient accounts payable process and inevitably more unnecessary work for the staff.

1. Does your organization issue Rush (ASAP) payments without backup? ___ Yes ___ No

2. Does your organization permit the return of checks to requisitioners? ___ Yes ___ No

3. Does your organization allow the same person to sign checks and approve invoices? ___ Yes ___ No

4. Does your organization allow the same person to process invoices and sign checks? ___ Yes ___ No

5. Does your organization allow the same person to print checks and sign checks? ___ Yes ___ No

6. Does your organization have the same person doing bank reconciliations and unclaimed property reporting? ___ Yes ___ No

7. Does your organization have a petty cash box? ___ Yes ___ No

8. Does your organization limit access to the master vendor file for the purposes of setting up new vendors? ___ Yes ___ No

9. Does your organization limit access to the master vendor file for the purposes of updating or changing vendor information? ___ Yes ___ No

10. Does your organization deactivate vendors in the master vendor file who have had no activity for the last 12 months? ___ Yes ___ No

11. Does your organization have a detailed written Travel & Entertainment policy? ___ Yes ___ No

12. Does your organization make managers responsible for all expense reimbursement reports they approve? ___ Yes ___ No

13. Does your organization enforce its Travel & Entertainment policy uniformly? ___ Yes ___ No

14. Does your organization immediately cancel credit cards of departing employees? ___ Yes ___ No

15. Does your organization insist that bank reconciliations be completed on a timely basis? ___ Yes ___ No

16. Is there management support for a policy of zero tolerance when it comes to policy abuse and/or fraud? ___ Yes ___ No

17. If your organization uses preprinted check stock, do you keep it under lock and key? ___ Yes ___ No

18. Does your organization insist that all employees involved even tangentially with payments take their vacations and during that time someone else performs their job functions? ___ Yes ___ No

19. Does your organization rotate jobs wherever possible, especially those of your processors? ___ Yes ___ No

20. Does your organization have a hotline where employees can anonymously report a suspected fraud? ___ Yes ___ No

Column A			**Column B**	
For questions 1-7	Total Yes	_______	Total No	_________
For questions 8-20	Total No	________	Total Yes	_________
Total Column A		________	**Total Column B**	________

See the following page for a discussion of the best practice responses.

Explanation of the Responses that Demonstrate Weak Controls

Let's compare the totals for Column A with the totals for Column B. Hopefully the Column A totals are much smaller than Column B, for those are the areas where you have potential weak spots. Now, let's take a look at why each issue creates a problem.

1. Issuing Rush (ASAP) payments without backup is an invitation to disaster in the form of duplicate payments and fraud. Yet, when a vendor screams or there is some other emergency, the number of organizations that rush the payment through without back-up is mindboggling.
2. Returning checks to requisitioners is one of the leading ways employees steal from their employers. While it is only the occasional employee who will dupe their employer this way, it is critical that this practice be eliminated. Additionally, a larger number than you might imagine of checks returned to requisitioners are misplaced.
3. Allowing the same person to sign checks and approve invoices does not employ requisite segregation of duties principles.
4. Allowing the same person to process invoices and sign checks does not employ requisite segregation of duties principles.
5. Allowing the same person to print checks and sign checks does not employ requisite segregation of duties principles.
6. Having the same person doing bank reconciliations and unclaimed property reporting does not employ requisite segregation of duties principles.
7. Petty cash boxes are an invitation to fraud and are an inefficient way to handle small dollar payments.
8. Not limiting access to the master vendor file for the purposes of setting up new vendors opens the door for a crook who wants to set up a phony vendor.
9. Not limiting access to the master vendor file for the purposes of updating or changing vendor information makes it easy for an employee to manipulate vendor data for their own gain.
10. Not deactivating vendors in the master vendor file who have had no activity for the last 12 months makes it easier for employees to mistakenly use the wrong vendor and to play games.
11. Not having a detailed written Travel & Entertainment policy makes it very difficult to rein in rogue employees who spend company funds on inappropriate items.
12. Not making managers responsible for all expense reimbursement reports they approve increases the likelihood that the manger will sign a report without looking at it. Employees who realize their superiors are not checking are more apt to stretch the rules.
13. Not enforcing the Travel & Entertainment policy uniformly leads to employee discontent and sometimes a pushing of the envelope.
14. Not immediately canceling credit cards of departing employees opens the organization open to unauthorized use. More than one organization has discovered to their dismay

that a few employees are not above using a company credit for personal purchases after they have left the organization, even if they left of their own accord.

15. Not doing bank reconciliation on a timely basis opens the organization up to an ongoing fraud that goes undetected for longer than it should.

16. Management support for a policy of zero tolerance when it comes to policy abuse and/or fraud strengthens an organization's controls and makes it clear to everyone that the organization will not tolerate misuse or fraud.

17. Keeping preprinted check stock under lock and key is a basic control when it comes to guarding against payment fraud. If check stock is left where anyone can take a few checks, the organization could find itself completely liable in the case of a check fraud.

18. Insisting that all employees involved even tangentially with payments take their vacations and during that time someone else performs their job functions is the best way to uncover an ongoing fraud. Usually, these vacations should be at least five consecutive days.

19. Job rotation wherever possible, is the best way to ensure an employee does not get too friendly with an employee at a vendor and collude with them for fraudulent purposes.

20. Since tips are one of the leading ways fraud is uncovered, having a hotline where employees can anonymously report a suspected fraud is considered to be a best practice.

So how'd you do? Very few organizations will end up with a completely clean bill of health when it comes to their internal controls so don't be overly concerned if you've identified two or three areas that need some revision. However, if you have more than a few of these less-than-stellar practices in your organization, you might want to take a serious look at revamping your procedures – quickly! **DIYAP**

The Silent AP Productivity Killers: How Many Do You Have?

Sometimes inadvertently we allow practices to slip into our workflow that make us less than efficient. In most cases these practices just eat into the profitability of the organization a little bit, but in a few they could mean the difference between showing a healthy profit or a dreaded loss.

The Productivity Killer Checklist begins on the next page.

AP Now's Productivity Killer Checklist

1) Do you allow Rush (ASAP) checks? ____ Yes ____ No
2) Do you permit the return of checks to requisitioners? ____ Yes ____ No
3) Do you have a petty cash box? ____ Yes ____ No
4) Does your organization require hand signatures on paper checks of low dollar amount? ____ Yes ____ No
5) Do you make unnecessary paper copies of documents? ____ Yes ____ No
6) Do you print invoices received electronically? ____ Yes ____ No
7) Do you produce reports no one uses? ____ Yes ____ No
8) Do you insist on doing all tasks in-house, outsourcing nothing including those that others can do at a lower cost and don't involve/require company/history knowledge? Examples include check printing, duplicate and erroneous payment audit recovery, vendor credit recovery etc. ____ Yes ____ No
9) Does your staff check every single T&E expense report by hand? ____ Yes ____ No
10) Do you regularly analyze staff productivity to ascertain who is not doing a good job? ____ Yes ____ No
11) Do you regularly retrain staff whose productivity is slipping? ____ Yes ____ No
12) Do you keep up to date on regulatory issues – information reporting, sales and use tax and unclaimed property? ____ Yes ____ No
13) Do you keep up on the newest frauds affecting businesses? ____ Yes ____ No
14) Do you keep up on the newest fraud prevention/detection services offered by your banks? ____ Yes ____ No
15) Do you regularly review staff work to make sure no one has introduced workarounds? ____ Yes ____ No
16) Does your organization require 100% policy compliance for T&E expenditures? ____ Yes ____ No
17) Does your organization get credit cards (both T&E and p-card) back from departing employees and cancel them immediately at the bank? ____ Yes ____ No
18) Do you periodically try to identify staff with hidden talents at handling difficult tasks – responding to vendor inquiries, resolving disputed invoices, etc. and assign work accordingly? ____ Yes ____ No
19) Does your organization try to get as many vendors as possible to accept ACH payments instead of paper checks? ____ Yes ____ No
20) Do you track which vendors have provided your organization with W-9s and which ones haven't? ____ Yes ____ No

Number of Yes Responses for Questions 1 -9 ____
Number of No Responses for Questions 10-20 ____

Total ____

Analysis of the Correct Responses

1 Ideally you will have written a zero on both lines and your sum would be zero. If that is the case you can skip the rest of the article. You are doing everything that you should be doing. However, we fear that very few will fall into that category. Most will have at least a few items that deserve further scrutiny. So, let's analyze the best practices that will help you avoid silently zapping the organization's productivity.

2

1. Allow more than the occasional Rush (ASAP) checks demonstrates poor internal controls. It is also the way some internal frauds are committed and many result in duplicate payments. The bottom line is this. Eliminate all but the few true emergency Rush checks and you'll not only have a more efficient (translation: lower costing) accounts payable function, you will also put a serious dent in potential duplicate payments.
2. The rational for not permitting the return of checks to requisitioners is the same as for not allowing Rush checks. If you get pushback on this issue, enlist the support of your auditors on this matter.
3. Likewise, a petty cash box should not be tolerated. In the current environment where p -cards and credit cards are a common phenomenon there really is no reason for most organizations to have a petty cash box. What's more they are an extremely inefficient way to pay for small expenditures and are frequently out of balance or worse.
4. Requiring hand signatures on paper checks of low dollar amount is a waste of time. Upfront controls should be tightened so manual signatures are only put on very large payments, if at all. Better yet, convert to ACH.
5. Look around at the desks of your staff. Are they covered in paper? How much of that paper is really necessary? Most organizations have unnecessary paper copies of documents all over the place.
6. Accepting invoices electronically and then printing them is just fooling yourself that you are accepting invoices electronically. Yes, you may be receiving them faster than you would otherwise, but you are leaving over half the productivity gains on the table by printing.
7. When was the last time you looked at the reports produced by your department? If they are not used to make meaningful decisions, then perhaps they are not worth the time spent producing them.
8. Outsourcing has become a four-letter word in many organizations. Yet there are times it does make sense. We're talking about those tasks that require specialized knowledge that others can do much better and more efficiently than your staff. Examples include check printing, duplicate and erroneous payment audit recovery, VAT reclaim, vendor credit recovery etc.
9. Checking every single T&E expense report by hand is an inefficient way to manage the travel and entertainment process. Spot checking combined with making managers responsible for what they approve is a better way to go.
10. Unless you regularly analyze staff productivity to ascertain who is not doing a good job, workers may pick up bad habits and become less productive. What's more, you may find that one or two of your staffers are extremely productive and by studying their work habits and processes you may be able to develop a more efficient way to handle the work flow.
11. By regularly retraining staff whose productivity is slipping, you will ensure the most productive accounts payable function possible.

12. Regulatory issues, including information reporting, sales and use tax and unclaimed property, require attention. What's needed changes from time to time and if you don't stay on top of these issues, you will suddenly find the organization needs to hire expensive consultants to get the company back on track. What's more, by ignoring the issues you may inadvertently subject the organization to penalties and fines.

13. Unfortunately, the number of crooks focused on the accounts payable function is growing as is their sophistication. For the most part, these are very smart people. If you do not keep up on the newest frauds affecting businesses, your organization could take a very bit hit indeed.

14. Likewise, you need to keep up on the newest fraud prevention/detection services offered by your banks. Otherwise you won't be able to combat the new fraud threats.

15. Creative staffers periodically figure out faster ways to do their job. Sometimes these shortcuts are good but more than occasionally they create problems elsewhere in the chain. Unless you regularly review staff work to make sure no one has introduced workarounds, you could have problems.

16. T&E policy compliance is as much a matter of corporate culture as it is internal controls. It is also something that is sometimes beyond the control of the department reviewing expense reports. Organizations that do not have 100% policy compliance for T&E expenditures face two productivity challenges. First, they end up spending more than they should on those who don't comply with the policy. And secondly, non-compliance by a few "favorites" encourages others to flout the policy, costing the organization a second time. Finally, it also leads to lower morale and there is a hidden cost there, as well.

17. Not getting credit cards (both T&E and p-card) back from departing employees and canceling them immediately at the bank can have unfortunate consequences should the employee decide to use the card for personal purchases. This simple task is often neglected in many organizations. The cards should be returned by the employee along with their employee badge and key during the exit interview. If this is not done, other routines should be incorporated into your processes to address this shortfall.

18. Very few managers periodically try and identify staff with hidden talents at handling difficult tasks – responding to vendor inquiries, resolving disputed invoices, etc. and assign work accordingly. This is an often overlooked strategy that can make the department run a lot smoother.

19. Paper checks are both costly and inefficient. Encouraging as many vendors as possible to accept ACH payments instead of paper checks will make the process a whole lot more effective.

20. While most organizations feel like they dodged a bullet when corporate reporting was repealed, we believe this is only temporary. The tax gap still exists and our legislators will be back in the not-too-distant future looking for ways to track those who are not paying their fair share. We've been warned. So by starting to track which vendors have provided your organization with W-9s and which ones haven't you will be ready when these ugly provisions are finally installed. What's more, if you are doing this and you end up with an IRS audit, you can demonstrate good intent by showing you are collecting and tracking W-9s.

So, how'd you do? Are there additional places you can tighten your processes? **DIYAP**

Looking for Fraud in All the Right Places

Usually when we talk about fraud in this publication, we focus on payment fraud. We also focus on tight internal controls and appropriate segregation of duties. By no means do we mean to underestimate the importance of those issues. But, unfortunately for the business world, there are other places where fraud can be uncovered in the payment arena. In this article we will look at ten of those that touch the accounts payable function and show you how to uncover the fraud hiding in the details of the transaction.

Hiding Place #1: Your vendor complaints. Do you investigate vendor complaints thoroughly, especially the ones that sound outlandish? Sometimes the complaints not only are legitimate they are a result of an employee playing games for their own enrichment. Of course, the perpetration of the fraud could be by the vendor so don't jump to conclusions right away.

Hiding Place #2: Your customer complaints. Just like the grievances of your vendors, your customers may have legitimate gripes caused by an ongoing fraud being committed by one of your employees. So, follow up and investigate closely. And, as with the vendor issues, it could be the customer trying to pull the wool over your eyes.

Hiding Place #3: Increased purchases from a particular vendor. An increase might reflect a kickback to one of your purchasing executives. To determine if the increase is substantial, compare average monthly purchases with the current month's purchases. Also, look at the prices being charged. Are they in line with what other vendors are charging? You might also want to consider whether another supplier of this produce has gone out of business or if a contract has been signed to purchase at a superior price. There's a lot of investigation that needs to go into this issue before you can determine if a fraud is in play.

Hiding Place #4: Questionable documentation. Unless there is an obvious reason, documentation for invoices should be original copies. If the documentation is obvious copies, you can question why. There may be a good reason, it could be a duplicate payment or worse, if could be fraud. The starting point is questioning the problematical documentation.

Hiding Place #5: Unusual endorsements on checks. If you get your checks returned from your bank, you can quickly thumb through the checks to see if any stand out as questionable. This might be an individual's signature on a corporate check. Most use a deposit stamp. If you don't get the checks, just the images, take a quick scan to see if anything jumps out and hits you as odd.

Hiding Place #6: Odd cancellation of vendor invoices. Some organizations cancel paper invoices after processing them. This might be with a hand stamp that says paid or with one of those machines that actually puts little holes through the invoices. If you use these approaches and find one with odd cancelations on it, look for a duplicate payment or worse, fraud.

Hiding Place #7: Altered or modified invoices. It's one thing to mark an invoice and pay a smaller amount than is due. It is a whole other issue if the invoice is marked up and a higher amount is put on the invoice for payment. Most organizations would not pay such an invoice requiring the vendor to send a revised invoice. Any invoice with handwritten or changes should be investigated closely. What's more, it is not a good idea to allow handwritten changes. For even if the change is legitimate, it sets a bad precedent and potentially opens the door for future fraud.

Hiding Place #8: Unusual payees. Hopefully a check written out to cash would set bells off for everyone reading this. But, more than that, checks other than payroll or expense reimbursement should also raise a red flag and be immediately investigated. The documentation for such checks, if they are legitimate, should be quite thorough and signed off by a senior manager.

Hiding Place #9: A different payee on the check register than the actual check. Clearly, this would be difficult to identify since most bank reconciliations are done by check number and dollar amount. Also, this problem is unlikely to occur with computer generated checks. If Rush checks are manually generated this might be possible. It is also the way most check fraud is committed today. The crook gets the check and knowing the organization uses positive pay, alters the payee name only. All differences should be investigated immediately.

Hiding Place #10: Unexpected changes in payables disbursements. This should be investigated immediately. It could be an error or it could be fraud. It needs to be identified and determined if the disbursement is correct. If not, action should be taken to retrieve the funds.

All of the issues discussed above require a thorough investigation before you decide there is fraud and an even more diligent investigation before you resolve who the guilty party is. But identifying the problem is the first step. We've given you some clues on where to look. The ball is now in your court as you decide how to proceed. **DIYAP**

Best Practice Advice: Segregation of Duties: How Much Access Do Your Employees *Really* Have?

How good is your segregation of duties assessments? There's an issue that often gets ignored and it affects segregation of duties. Does your organization actively encourage promoting from within? Many do and to be honest Accounts Payable Now & Tomorrow thinks it's a great idea. When you hire from within you get an employee who knows the organization, has a proven track record as well as one who knows and understands the corporate culture. However, if you do not take the right steps, you could unintentionally create a segregation of duties nightmare.

The Potential Scenario

Now, we are going to concede right up front, that we are presenting a worst case scenario. We are doing this simply to make the point, not that we think this situation is commonplace. Let's say someone joins your accounts payable department in the most junior level invoice processing position. They are given access to enter invoices in your computer system. That is all. After a few years of sterling performance, the person is promoted and now is responsible for printing checks. They are given access to the check creation part of the process.

After a year or two of thanklessly printing checks for the organization, they are promoted to handle your master vendor file. They set up new vendors and make changes where needed to existing vendors.
Do you see the problem? If the employees' access to the system is not terminated when they leave each job and move to the next, you now have an employee who can create a vendor in the master vendor file, process an invoice and print a check.

The Solution

Clearly, we need to cut employees access whenever they leave a job. This means not only when they leave the company but also when they move to a new position within the organization. Just imagine how many accesses an employee who has been with an organization for 20 years might have.

The above suggestion solves the issue going forward. But what about the mess you might have on your hands now? A report should be run showing what access each employee has. It should be matched against what access is required by the person's current position.
Once you've uncovered your list of extra accesses review it carefully. Before automatically cutting everyone's unneeded access, let them know what you are doing. You should except to get some flak from some of the folks on the list. Just because they are not supposed to have access doesn't mean they aren't using their unauthorized access. It might make their job easier or they may be supplying information to others higher up in the organization.

It is a good idea to run this report once a year just to make sure the segregation of duties is complete and no problems have crept in. Similarly, it is smart for those who normally terminate access to run the report to make sure it is always done.

As you probably realize, this is not just an accounts payable issue but one that affects all departments within your organization. If you find problems with extra accesses in accounts payable, you might want to bring the issue to the attention of the controller and/or CFO as it is likely the problem is not a local one but one potentially affecting every department within the firm. **DIYAP**

Best Practice Advice: Five Ways to Protect *Your* Organization From Payment Fraud

Whenever I talk to controllers, CFOs, and accounts payable directors and managers, I'm amazed that most seem to think that payment fraud is something that happens to the other guy—not something they really need to concern themselves about. I'm always tempted to scream at them: *wrong*! But now I don't have to. A survey by the Association for Financial Professionals (AFP) provides the metrics that make the case. Payment fraud is *always* an issue for accounts payable and now that hard economic times have fallen on many, we need to ramp up our defenses.

How Bad Is the Problem?

To begin with, 72 percent of organizations experienced attempted or actual payments fraud in 2006. What's worse, 39 percent reported that incidence of fraud had increased from the prior year. That's in one year. And in 2006 the economy was humming along (although, as we now know, we were right on the precipice readying for the fall).

It will probably come as no surprise to our readers to learn that checks are still the preferred target and almost all organizations that had attempted fraud had some cases of attempted (or actual) check fraud. Yet another reason, perhaps, to move away from paper checks.

However, moving entirely away from paper checks won't completely solve the problem. Slightly over one-third had problems with ACH debits and another 14% had problems with corporate purchasing cards.

While checks may account for the lion's share of the problems, no one can afford to ignore controls around their other payment vehicles.

Check Fraud

Many crooks, unfortunately, are not stupid; they know about positive pay. The most common type of check fraud is altered payee names on checks issued. Almost two thirds of the respondents had to deal with this issue. Like virtually every other expert, *Accounts Payable Now & Tomorrow* advises all its readers to use positive pay—and as you will shortly see, payee name positive pay if your bank has that product available. (The accompanying chart provides definitions of some of the terms used in this article.)

> *AP Now recommendation:* If you have not recently reviewed the controls you have around your check stock, check signing procedures, where you keep checks awaiting hand signatures, and how and when you mail your checks, this might be a good time to do so.

The next most common type of check fraud demonstrates just how technologically advanced some fraudsters are. Almost 60% had to deal with crooks taking MICR line information from a check and using it under a different organization's name.

AP Now recommendation: For starters, use a separate account for wire transfers and only give out wiring information if you are 100% certain that the person on the other end of the phone is entitled to the data. Additionally, set up a separate account for refunds and other monies returned to customers. Overpaying for a small item and waiting for the refund check is another way thieves get your accounts numbers. And of course, lost, stolen, and counterfeit checks continue to be a problem for just over 40%.

AP Now recommendation: Encourage direct deposit of payroll wherever possible. Unfortunately, many states still forbid companies from mandating the use of this service.

Of course, the best way to limit your exposure to check fraud is to stop using paper checks. But, when you do, make sure you incorporate strong controls in your new processes so you don't end up trading one problem for another.

ACH Fraud

Slightly over one-third (36%) of the AFP respondents said they had experienced ACH fraud or had it attempted against them. This is through the use of ACH debits. There are some easy protections offered by virtually every financial institution that facilitates ACH debits. Simply put an ACH block or filter on your accounts, whichever is applicable. While not quite as good as positive pay these two weapons go a long way towards thwarting this type of crime.

AP Now recommendation: If you are not currently permitting ACH debits, put an ACH block on every single bank account your organization has. Remember to remove them should you decide at some point to allow ACH debits.

Additionally, if you are going to allow ACH debits, concentrate this activity in a limited number of accounts.

Card Payment Fraud

Most of the fraud surrounding card payment fraud occurred when organizations accepted consumer credit cards. While this is good news for those advocating the use of a corporate procurement card, it doesn't mean you can let your guard down when it comes to p-cards. Over one-quarter (27%) indicated corporate cards were the second most frequent source of card payments fraud.

This could occur because the employee misuses the card or because a fraudster got his or her mitts on the card number. There are many ways to limit losses here. Daily limits, MCC restrictions, end-user training, frequent reviews and approvals are just some of the commonsense best practices that will help combat fraud.

AP Now recommendation: Perhaps the most overlooked best practice relates to how p-cards are handled when an employee leaves the organization, regardless of who instigated the change. Accounts payable and the bank should be notified immediately and the card cancelled. Make returning the card part of your exit process, just as you might get keys back. This is probably the most overlooked fraud prevention technique—and it costs nothing.

Best Practices to Prevent Payment Fraud

The Association of Fraud Examiners in their biannual Report to the Nation provides statistics on a whole range of fraud issues. Year after year it finds that internally, fraud is most frequently committed by long-term, trusted, employees. This fact bears mentioning once again. Frequently organizations implement a series of stringent procedures to ensure appropriate controls only to ruin them by making it possible for one trusted employee to violate them.

7) Auditors can find documents themselves, freeing the accounts payable staff of that onerous task. All you'll have to do is point them in the right direction.

In fact, the AFP survey notes that, "Internal fraud appears to be an important factor in check and ACH fraud as well, and one of the reasons why organizations must assume liability for financial losses from the fraud."

So, when all is said is and done, what should you do to protect your organization? The AFP has some excellent advice for our readers. "Organizations can accomplish a great deal toward safeguarding their financial transactions," they say, "by increased adoption of fraud control services, greater attention to internal procedures, and expanded use of electronic payments for vendor and employee pay." We wholeheartedly agree. **DIYAP**

Management Issues: Operation Issues

- The Duplicate Payment and Recovery Best Practice Checklist
- Policy & Procedures Manual Checklist
- Launching a New Project Best Practice Checklist
- Best Practice Advice: A Marriage Made in Heaven: 10 Reasons to Put Imaging in Your Technology Upgrade
- ¨Best Practice Advice: Electronic AP: Eight Simple Tactics Any Company Can Use
- Best Practice Advise: Eight Tried-and-Tested Strategies to Help Any AP Department Save Time
- Best Practice Advice: Change in Accounts Payable: A 5 Step Plan to Maximize Your Resources

Duplicate Payment Prevention and Recovery Best Practices Check-list

1) Do you have strict coding standards for invoices? ____ Yes ____ No

2) Do you have a naming standard for the master vendor file? ___ Yes ____ No

3) Do you periodically check vendor statements looking for open credits? ____ Yes ____ No

4) Do you insist on backup for all check request forms? ____ Yes ____ No

5) Do you periodically review old Rush check requests to make sure the invoice wasn't paid later? ____ Yes ____ No

6) Do you review invoices paid very late to make sure they weren't previously paid? ____ Yes ____ No

7) Do you return invoices without an invoice number to the vendor requesting an invoice with an invoice number? ____ Yes ____ No

8) Do you insist on using only one payment vehicle per vendor? ____ Yes ____ No

9) If you allow more than one payment vehicle per vendor, do you review their payment histories periodically? ____ Yes ____ No

10) Do you make sure that payments made outside accounts payable use the same rigid processing standards used in accounts payable? _ ___ Yes ____ No

Total ______ Yes ______ No

A discussion of the best responses is on the following page.

A Discussion of the Duplicate Payment and Recovery Best Practice Checklist

Clearly a yes was the desired response to each of the questions on the checklist. Let's take a look at why.

1. A strict coding standard for invoices is proven to be one of the very best ways to eliminate duplicate payments. Once one is developed it is imperative that it be shared with all processors and they all use it all the time.
2. A naming standard for the master vendor file will ensure that duplicate entries to the master vendor file are not created. Again, this will go a long way towards insuring that a second invoice does not get paid.
3. Periodically requesting vendor statements showing <u>all</u> activity is a great way not only to identify duplicate payments but also find unused open credits. When you find them, research their genesis to ensure you close the loopholes that allowed them to happen in the first place.
4. By insisting on backup for all check request forms you greatly decrease the chance of making a duplicate payment. Too often these requests have nothing on them other than the payee name, the dollar amount and the authorizing signature. This is an invitation to a duplicate.
5. Too often, when a Rush check (for a missing invoice) is issued and the backup for the transaction is limited or nonexistent, the original invoice is paid when it finally shows up in accounts payable. As discussed elsewhere in this issue, if POs and receiving docs are not extinguished there is no way for accounts payable to know that the invoice actually was paid. By periodically reviewing old Rush check requests you can find those duplicates yourself, instead of letting a third party auditor find them and charge a fee for its services.
6. Really late invoices were more than occasionally paid with a Rush check. Any time an invoice with an old date shows up, check your records to make sure it hasn't been already paid. And don't just rely on the invoice number. Look for the dollar amount as well. Remember those Rush check requests with no backup.
7. Since invoice number is often a key factor in determining if an invoice has already been paid, returning invoices without invoice numbers to the vendor requesting they include an invoice number on this and all future invoices is a great way to minimize the problem.
8. Too often, duplicate payments arise when a vendor is paid twice using different payment vehicles, say a p-card and a check. By limiting each vendor to only one payment vehicle the risk of making a duplicate payment via that error is eliminated.
9. Occasionally, it is not possible to limit a vendor to one payment vehicle. The payment histories of these vendors should periodically be checked to ensure they were not paid twice for the same item.
10. When payments are made outside accounts payable insist the unit making the payment uses the same rigid processing standards used in accounts payable. Otherwise, duplicates and other erroneous payments will slip in. **DIYAP**

How Good Is Your Policy and Procedures Manual?

When it comes to running an efficient, effective, fraud-resistant, regulatory compliant accounts payable function, an updated policy and procedures manual is critical. Not only does it lay the foundation for how the work of the department is to be completed, it serves as a valuable resource tool should a worker have a procedural problem. Yet, many organizations don't have a good manual in place. Do you? Use AP Now's Policy and Procedures Manual Diagnostic to figure out if your manual needs just a minor tweaking or a major overhaul.

1. Do you have a policy and procedures manual for the accounts payable function? ___ Yes ___ No
2. Has it been reviewed and updated within the last 12 months? ___ Yes ___ No
3. Does the manual accurately reflect the way your processors handle invoices? ___ Yes ___ No
4. Does the manual clearly spell out your cut off dates? ___ Yes ___ No
5. Has your manual been reviewed and updated to ensure it complies with IRS guidelines for 1099 Reporting? ___ Yes ___ No
6. Has your manual been reviewed and updated to ensure it complies with IRS guidelines for reporting payments made to foreign suppliers? ___ Yes ___ No
7. Has your manual been reviewed and updated to ensure it complies with current sales and use tax guidelines? ___ Yes ___ No
8. Has your manual been reviewed and updated to ensure it complies with current unclaimed property reporting and remitting laws? ___ Yes ___ No
9. Has you manual been reviewed and updated to ensure your internal controls are strong and appropriate? ___ Yes ___ No
10. Has your manual been reviewed and updated to ensure proper segregation of duties are being employed in the entire payment function? ___ Yes ___ No
11. Have you given each processor a copy of the manual? ___ Yes ___ No
12. Do you make sure all processors and other affected parties get copies of all updates to the policy? ___ Yes ___ No
13. If T&E are included in your policy and procedures manual, have those sections been reviewed to ensure they meet IRS guidelines for accountable plans? ___ Yes ___ No
14. Does your policy and procedures manual address backup procedures in case of unexpected absences? ___ Yes ___ No
15. Have you made any changes since the last update that are not reflected in the manual? ___ Yes ___ No

A Discussion of the Best Practice Responses

Clearly the correct answer to all the questions was yes, with the exception of the last item which ideally was answered no. Let's take a look at the correct responses and why they are recommended.

1. One of the first steps to employing best practices in any accounts payable operation is to have a policy and procedures manual detailing the procedures used in the department. Without it, processors have to guidelines.

2. The policy and procedures manual is not a static document. It needs to be changed to reflect the changing workflow. And the way things have been changing in the last few years, reviewing and updating within the last 12 months will keep your manual from getting out of date. Those who review and update it even more frequently are to be commended.

3. A manual is only worthwhile if it accurately reflect the way your processors handle invoices. Too often people download one off the Internet. What they end up with is a manual that reflects another organization's practices. If you do download one, you can make it your own by modifying it to reflect your practices. But be forewarned, that can entail a lot of work. It will not be as easy as making a few minor changes.

4. One of the important functions of an accounts payable policy and procedures manual is to clearly spell out your cut off dates. This information is important not only to those who work in accounts payable, but also those who submit items for payment. Share your cut-off schedule generously; it will help avoid problems.

5. The manual should be reviewed and updated to ensure it complies with IRS guidelines for 1099 Reporting. This is becoming an increasingly important issue. So, treat 1099s with the same attention and care you give the rest of the function. And, it is critical your procedures conform to IRS guidelines. This is not a place to take shortcuts.

6. Similarly, if you have foreign vendors, your manual should be reviewed and updated to ensure it complies with IRS guidelines for reporting payments made to foreign suppliers.

7. And, yes, the manual needs to be reviewed and updated to ensure it complies with current sales and use tax guidelines.

8. Unclaimed property is just as important as the other regulatory issues. Your manual should be reviewed and updated to ensure it complies with current unclaimed property reporting and remitting laws.

9. By reviewing your manual to ensure your internal controls are strong and appropriate, you are killing two birds with one stone. Shortfalls reflected in the manual highlight a need to tighten controls and revise current procedures.

10. Along the same line, reviewing your manual to ensure proper segregation of duties are being employed in the entire payment function will spotlight potential problems in your current procedures.

11. Each processor should have a copy of the manual or online access to it so they can use it any time they have a question about how to handle a particular issue. The

manual is meant to be shared and used.

12. There's no sense updating the manual if you don't make sure all processors and other affected parties get copies of all updates to the policy. So, send around updates to anyone who might need to know.

13. Some organizations include their Travel & Entertainment policy in their accounts payable manual. If so, it should be reviewed to ensure it meets IRS guidelines for accountable plans.

14. The policy and procedures manual needs to focus not only on the day-to-day issues but also backup procedures in case of unexpected absences. By laying out ahead of time what should be done when someone is unexpectedly not there, you'll avoid a lot of the tension and havoc that can accompany these occasions.

15. Making changes in the procedures and not reflecting them immediately in the manual is an invitation to disaster. When manuals were printed and the distribution was a big deal, there was an excuse. But with manual being posted online or distributed as pdf or Word files, there is no excuse for not immediately updating the manual and sharing the information. **DIYAP**

Are You *Really* Ready to Launch that New Project?

Determining ahead of time whether your new project is doomed to fail or on planted firmly on the road to success is something every smart manager takes into consideration before beginning a new project. If you're on the failure route, you can identify the trouble spots and take the appropriate steps to remedy the situation. Use our checklist below to determine which route your project is likely to take.

1. Have you defined exactly what you want to achieve with this program, defining your goals in hard numbers that can be measured? ___ Yes ___ No

2. Do you have a corporate sponsor, a high level executive who supports and champions the project? ___ Yes ___ No

3. Have you factored into your plans the likelihood that there will be resistance to the changes your new project will require? ___ Yes ___ No

4. Have you set a realistic timeframe for the completion of the project, allowing some extra time for those inevitable problems that will pop up? ___ Yes ___ No

5. Have you arranged for adequate employee training so the new project will not fail due to employee errors? ___ Yes ___ No

6. Have you factored in incentives for employees to make the changes the new project will require? ___ Yes ___ No

7. Have you included regular updates to management on the progress of the project as part of your overall strategy? ___ Yes ___ No

8. Have you talked with others who have implemented the technology (if it is a technology project) or made similar changes to find out what problems they encountered when

their project went live? ___ Yes ___ No

9. Have you tried to adjust your project to address the problems your peers encountered when they launched the same or similar projects? ___ Yes ___ No

10. Have you identified employees likely to object to your project and tried to get them onboard ahead of time? ___ Yes ___ No

11. Have you evaluated outside relationships (customers, suppliers etc.) to determine if any of them will be impacted by your change? ___ Yes ___ No

12. If you've determined that any of your outside relationships will be affected, have you made plans to incorporate their concerns into the project? ___ Yes ___ No

13. Have you done a cost benefit analysis to ensure your project makes financial sense? ___ Yes ___ No

14. Have you investigated how your changes are likely to affect other departments? ___ Yes ___ No

15. Have you addressed with those affected by the changes likely to be required by your new project, how they can adapt? ___ Yes ___ No

16. Do you have the full support from your immediate supervisor for this project? ___ Yes ___ No

17. Is there a project that your immediate supervisor deems more urgent that this one? ___ Yes ___ No

18. Do you have someone on staff capable of taking on the project important to your supervisor? ___ Yes ___ No

19. Are you able to reassign work within the department so the person assigned the project will be able to take in on and complete it within the agreed upon timeframe? ___ Yes ___ No

20. If you don't have someone capable on staff, has management given you adequate funding to hire someone for the needed period of time to complete it for you? ___ Yes ___ No

Best Practice Responses to the New Project Success/Failure Checklist

As you've probably figured out, the best practice answer for every question was Yes. If any of these issues are ignored the chances for project failure increase. Whether you are reengineering your accounts payable function or just a small part of it or implementing a massive new technology in the department, the issues are basically the same. Let's take a look at the reasoning behind the checklist.

1. If you don't have an exact idea of what project success looks like, you'll never know if you achieved it. What's more, you won't be able to prove to management that the project went well. By defining exactly what you want to achieve with this program, defining your goals in hard numbers that can be measured everyone will be on the same page and have the same expectations. There will be no miscommunication on this is-

sue.

2. Don't underestimate the value of a corporate sponsor, a high level executive who supports and champions the project. When you get pushback from other departments or employees, his or her support will be critical to keep your project from going off the rails. While it is theoretically possible to have a successful project without such a sponsor, the odds of success are much higher with one.

3. It's a fact of life unfortunately, that a certain subset of people don't react well to change – even if it's for the better. Be prepared for the naysayers across all levels of the company. They will put up a fuss. That's part of the reason having a corporate sponsor is so important. You'll be able to shut some of them down just be mentioning the corporate sponsor's name. Others will take a little more convincing.

4. At the beginning of a project, especially if it's one you waited a long time to launch, it's easy to be over optimistic about how long it will take to complete. This is especially true if new technology is involved. Set a realistic timeframe for the completion of the project, allowing some extra time for those inevitable problems that will pop up. It's much better to finish early and look like a hero than finish late making excuses as to why the project was delayed.

5. Many of the projects related to accounts payable result in a change in procedures. This is especially true when new technology is involved. If adequate employee training for these changes is not included in the plan, the new project will not fail due to employee errors and inability to use the new process/technology correctly.

6. Sometimes, when starting a new project, you are so focused on the benefits for the accounts payable function, you forget about the impact it will have on others. If you can show incentives for employees who have to make the changes, they are much more likely to go along. Never forget the what's-in-it-for-them issue when promoting your new project.

7. Forgetting to regular update management on a regular basis on the progress of the project is one of the best ways to ensure disaster. Keep the project in front of their eyes hopefully pointing out how you are ahead of plan or at least on target. Should there be a problem, bring it to their attention and explain what you are doing to rectify the matter. Otherwise, you run the risk of having someone who is against the project presenting the problem in the worst possible light.

8. Learning from others' mistakes is a great way to avoid problems that don't appear obvious at first glance. By talking with others who have implemented the technology (if it is a technology project) or made similar changes you can find out what problems they encountered when their project went live.

9. Once you've identified the issues encountered by your peers, adjust your project to address the problems they encountered when they launched the same or similar projects. This won't completely eliminate all problems, but it will help you avoid some of them.

10. By identifying employees likely to object to your project and trying to get them onboard ahead of time you will avoid a lot of headaches. If you enlist their support and get them to see the benefits of the new project, they could end up being your biggest supporters.

11. It's not only insiders who may have to change, but sometimes your new project will

affect outsiders. This can be ugly if they refuse to go along so it is critical that you identify such cases and evaluate outside relationships (customers, suppliers etc.) to determine if any of them will be impacted by your change.

12. Once you have determined there will be some impact, it is equally important to plan how you will address it. You don't want to lose either customers or critical vendors over a change made in accounts payable.

13. A new program can have wonderful benefits, but if your organization can't afford it, there's little sense in advocating for it. Doing a cost benefit analysis to ensure your project makes financial sense before plunging headfirst is not only good from a business standpoint, it is also smart from a career point of view.

14. Other departments may have to change how they handle their workflow. By identifying those functions early on, you'll be one step ahead.

15. Once you've identified those departments or functions affected, it is imperative that you a discussion with them to work out how they will address the changes. If you don't they could refuse to change negating all your efforts

16. Don't overlook the impact your immediate supervisor can have on this project. If this is a project that came to you through other channels, your supervisor could feel left out or marginalized. Make sure to regularly update her/him, keep them in the loop and include them wherever possible.

17. The immediate supervisor issue can get even dicier if he/she has a project she/he deems more urgent that the one you are working on. It doesn't matter which is more important; this is an issue with political overtones. If you can possibly take on the second project do so. If not, discuss the issue with your supervisor and perhaps ask to work on it as soon as the current project is completed. Don't ignore it if it is important to your supervisor. It could be the sleeper issue that derails your current project.

18. Another way to address the supervisor issue is to perhaps have someone else on staff take on the project. Hopefully, this approach will make everyone happy.

19. Nothing will doom a project faster than assigning it to a capable person who already has their plate full. If at all possible, unless it is a small project, reassign work within the department so the person assigned the project will be able to take in on and complete it within the agreed upon timeframe.

20. Alternatively, if you don't have someone capable on staff, ask management to give you adequate funding to hire someone for the needed period of time to complete it for you. They can work on the project or the extra staff work, whichever works better for the organization as a whole.

Special projects are an important component of any accounts payable function that is looking to change. In the environment we operate in today, change is a constant. By making sure you address all the potential landmines, you will have a much greater chance for success with your new projects. **DIYAP**

Best Practice Advice: Electronic AP: Eight Simple Tactics Any Company Can Use

Perhaps the biggest change to the accounts payable function over the last few years is the rate that it is being automated. I'm not just talking about big company high-dollar automation projects. We're also talking about low-dollar, process changes that every company can implement without spending a fortune—and in many cases without spending a single red cent. Let's take a look at some of these strategies.

1. Get rid of paper invoices. Next to paper checks, paper invoices are the biggest time consumer in accounts payable. And that doesn't even address the issue of storage. Even if you don't sign up for a third party e-invoicing service, you can accept invoices by email. Many suppliers are refusing to mail invoices and accepting them by email should be a no-brainer. Don't give back your savings by printing the invoices once they arrive in your shop. Establish standard procedures for processing them without the paper.
2. Eliminate those paper faxed invoices and other faxes by signing up for a low cost e-fax facility that converts your paper faxes to emails so you never again get a fax delivered on paper. This is another tactic that will help eliminate paper invoices from the accounts payable department.
3. When you have to send documents, either for approval or because there is a dispute, don't make copies and mail them. Scan the documents and attach them to emails for discussion or resolution. Of course, if you received the documents electronically, you won't have to scan them.
4. Encourage vendors to accept payments via the ACH instead of receiving paper checks. This will not only reduce the amount of paper, it will save tons of processing time – and of course, save a few trees. Best of all ACH payments are cheaper than issuing a paper check and rarely result in an unclaimed property obligations.
5. Insist on ACH for all employee reimbursements for expenses. While most states won't allow you to mandate electronic payments for payroll, you can insist on reimbursing employees for expenses this way.
6. Email your vendors receiving ACH payments their remittance information. If you can find an effective way to do this, more vendors will sign up for your ACH program, eliminating even more of those awful paper checks. One of the main reasons suppliers are reluctant to sign up for ACH is the lack of information usually included on the remittance advice and used to apply cash. If you can find a way to deliver that information to the person responsible for applying cash, you will have won that battle.
7. Only make Rush payments using the ACH. Do not issue checks outside the normal check production schedule. This can be a tough one but once the vendor receives the payment in their bank account the very next day, they will find they like it and may switch to receiving all payments from you electronically. Paying via the ACH will eliminate some—but not all—of the problems associated with Rush checks.
8. Purchase a low-cost simple scanner for use in handling those documents that do arrive in paper format. Scan the invoices before distributing them to your processors for handling. Let them learn to process invoices without relying on that piece of paper. This will make it easier if you go one day to a third party e-invoicing process. And, it will save on storage.

So, how many of these tactics are you already using and how many could you work into your current processes? There really is no excuse for not getting started. **DIYAP**

Best Practice Advice: A Marriage Made in Heaven: 10 Reasons to Put Imaging in Your Technology Upgrade Plan

With the price of imaging technology dropping and increasingly available on a pay-as-you-go basis it's time to reevaluate the technology for use in your accounts payable function. It's been a rough few years for managers trying to get budget allocations for technology but with the first glimmers of the light at the end of the recovery tunnel, imaging may finally get the adoption rate it deserves.

You often see the pay-as-you-go services referred to as SaaS (software as a service) and this approach is enjoying growing acceptance, especially given the budget constraints over the last few years. So here are a few reasons you may want to take another look at imaging.

1) It improves processing time giving your staff greater ability to focus on exception items and other value-added tasks. And we will be up-front about another result of the adoption of imaging: some departments have been able to reduce headcount in accounts payable due its introduction.

2) Departmental efficiency is likely to improve as processors are no longer responsible for keying in invoices and can focus their attention instead on the accuracy of the information not the data entry.

3) You'll say goodbye to lost early payment discounts, the best investment alternative for any organization. However, to earn them you need to process invoices quickly. What better way to get that process started than to eliminate the data entry and mail time? Invoices can be sent immediately to the AP department for prompt processing.

4) Imaging will drastically reduce the time your processors spend retrieving documents from filing cabinets when they need to refer to them. Additionally, the documents will always be filed away where they should be. Misfiling becomes a thing of the past.

5) No more worries about documents taken from the files and never returned or misfiled when and if they *are* put back. It happens in every organization—in fact, a few lock their documents to keep out employees in other departments who plunder the files when they need to see invoices.

6) You'll be able to eliminate those rows and rows of file cabinets and reduce storage space.

7) Auditors can find documents themselves, freeing the accounts payable staff of that onerous task. All you'll have to do is point them in the right direction.

8) Imaging creates an audit trail helping auditors and processors alike.

9) Difficult invoices won't get "lost." It becomes impossible for a processor to throw away or hide an invoice that they just can't seem to get resolved. Not, of course, that this ever happens in *your* shop—just at other organizations.

10) Imaging can help improve the sometimes-frayed relationships with other departments. When combined with workflow, imaging ends the "he "said, she said" games

that sometimes go on between accounts payable and purchasing. The electronic audit trail makes finger-pointing difficult—it's just too easy to find out what really happened.

There are numerous other reasons imaging is attractive; these are simply the main ones affecting accounts payable. If the imaging discussion has been off limits in your organization, use this article to put it back on the table. **DIYAP**

Best Practice Advise: Eight Tried-and-Tested Strategies to Help Any AP Department Save Time

With too much work and not enough resources, any tactic that enables an overworked accounts payable department to save even ten minutes is welcome. Those ten minute time savers add up and before you know it, you've found an extra hour to work on that project that keeps getting pushed to the bottom of your To-Do list. What follows are seven tactics used by readers in their own departments.

1. GL Codes when Setting up New Vendors

Include a field on your new vendor setup form for the general ledger (GL) code that is generally used for that vendor. This saves time keying in the GL code. It will show up automatically when invoices are entered. Processors are cautioned that the code is not set in stone and if they get a transaction that should be coded differently; they can override the standard GL code.

2. Faster Approvals on Early Pay Discount Invoices

Early payment discounts are the best investment alternative any organization has. But, unfortunately, many lose them because they fail to get those invoices approved on a timely basis. This doesn't have to be. Identify invoices with early payment discounts available and code them for special tracking. Set up your system so it will send alerts for invoices coming due with discounts that could be lost if not approved immediately.

3. Automatic Coding on Repetitive Invoices

Do you get invoices from the same vendor for the same items over and over again? Most of us do. If you are using one of the new e-payable systems, you may be able to take advantage of this fact to simplify GL coding. Many have a feature that codes invoices that have the same coding every time and sends them straight to the approver.

4. Reducing Invoice Copies

Do you find your staff is making copies of the same invoice over and over again to send to various departments that might need a copy? Here's a simpler way. Set up a dedicated email address and scan directly to it for required copies of invoices which have been expensed to pre-paid accounts and capital projects. No more making backup copies for the accountants. Just scan the invoices directly to each email address that is set up in the copier/scanner. This idea has saved us time and paper.

5. Printing Electronic Invoices

As much as it pains us to report this, some accounts payable departments print invoices received by email. If you must do this, this tip will help. Print all invoices in one fell swoop instead of as the emails are received. Set aside a time to do this, either first thing in the morning for all invoices received electronically within the last 24 hours or perhaps at the end of the day when some of your staff might be operating on less than 100% efficiency. This can be a huge time saver if you receive many invoices by e-mail which must then be printed.

6. Lock the Formulas

Every once in a while, an employee will decide to play games with their expense reimbursement requests. While Excel was the answer to those awful Xeroxed forms used twenty or more years ago, it does have its flaws. It is not as ironclad as you might like, unless you take some additional steps. If your company uses an Excel spreadsheet for expense reports, make sure it's a version that includes formulas and is locked for editing (with a password!). Employees submitting reimbursement should not be able to insert or delete rows, change formula cells, or insert their own mileage reimbursement amount. Doing so will save a ton of time and help keep your employees on the straight and narrow – whether they want to be or not.

7. Using Variances

When the three-way match doesn't work, it means a lot of extra work for the processor handling the invoice. This is fine when the discrepancy is a significant amount of money. But, when it's a very small amount, as it often is, resolving the discrepancy is not the best use of the processor's time. Not to mention, the time wasted on the vendor's side and in your purchasing department. Work with the controller and purchasing departments to determine a maximum tolerance for variances. This could include a percent as well as a dollar amount. i.e.: Prices and/or receipt overages could vary by 5%, but no more than $20. Otherwise, the purchasing department would be contacted to discuss the variances, and update the PO or dispute with the vendor accordingly. This should be written into a formal memo or policy. This policy could also include freight charges if separate approval is required for freight costs.

8. Making Maximum Use of Your Software

How often have you received a report and then had to get out your calculator to do some basic arithmetic to get the information you really needed? Or do you get reports and then have to search madly through a few pages to find the data you want because the information isn't sorted in a meaningful way. Take advantage of your computer and before printing reports next time, take a look and see if you can get some simple help from the computer. Adding totals to reports that didn't have them (that seems a given but there are usually a number of reports that don't have totals), doing sorts on reports to present information in a better way, downloading information into Excel rather than printing a report, developing queries to get the information faster and more straightforward, accessing information on screen more easily and directly, etc. Any time the computer can be used to get what is needed or make an improvement, it's used. **DIYAP**

Maximize Your Resources

If you are like many other professionals, your organization has a list of process improvements it would like to make, but has limited time and resources to implement those changes. Sometimes the sheer number of potential projects is so overwhelming that none of them get worked on. What's worse is when a few get started but resources are so thin that none get finished. This makes the accounts payable department look completely ineffectual. What follows is a five step plan any organization can use to effect change in its accounts payable function.

Step 1: Selecting the Right Project

Begin by making a list of all the projects you'd like to undertake. If you are just getting started, you want to focus on some projects that will be successful rather than those that will require monumental efforts. Once you've completed the list, eliminate those that will require a financial investment that is more than your organization is likely to make. This number will vary from company to company. For some it may be $1 million while for others it could be $10,000. You can move them to the bottom of the list or put them on a "For Future Consideration" list.

Next remove from consideration that projects that you expect to be a huge political battle. For some it might be a controller who is dead set against a p-card program and for others it might be a purchasing group adamant about getting invoices first.
Once you've gotten rid of the projects which would be difficult to get off the ground, focus on those that will improve the efficiency of your department the most. Narrow that list down to two or three and then start with the one you expect to be the easiest to complete. Your goal, if you are just getting started, is to have some successes.

Step 2: Starting in the Right Place

Once you've selected the project, you want to give it the best chance possible of being a success. You don't want some naysayer to roadblock it before you have a chance to get out of the gate. So, find a good starting point: the person/department/vendors most likely to adopt the change.

This is someone (department or vendor) who will work with you through the learning bumps. So, for example, if you want to start paying electronically, select a few test vendors that you have good relationships with and/or who have been asking for payments electronically. They are less likely to shut down if the process doesn't go smoothly the first time out of the gate. If they've got experience in this area, say electronic payments, they may also be able to share some advice of pitfalls to avoid.

Step 3: Don't Forget the WIFFM for your Partner

Sometimes we get so focused on how something will improve accounts payable, we forget about the other guy, the "what's in it for me" for them. Don't overlook the benefits for the end user or partner, especially if they are going to have to change the way they handle a certain task or process.

While this might not be critical in the first phase when you are working with people sympathetic to your project but it will become increasingly important as you try and line up additional support and take the program live.

Step 4: Fine Tune before Rolling out To the Large Audience

No matter how hard you try, you won't get everything 100% right. It's just the way it goes. It is critical that you get feedback from the early adopters and adjust the program accordingly. Get in-depth input from them. While they may be willing to live with minor inconveniences, especially if the process is something they wanted, your audience at large generally will not and will use the shortcomings as an excuse not to adopt your change.
Take the suggestions from your first group and adjust accordingly so the rest of your audience will have no excuse not to adopt the new process.

Step 5: Roll out to Everyone

Once everything has been smoothed out, roll out to the larger audience. Your new process needs to be the one used by everyone. If it is not, the effectiveness of your new program will be diminished greatly. So, don't let anyone slip through the cracks if you can possibly help it.

This will mean regular follow up to get the laggards on board.

What's next?

Once you've successfully rolled out an initiative, you are not done. This is not the time to rest on your laurels. If management is pleased with the way the project unfolded the time is ripe to get started on your next project.
Go back to step one and start again. After you've successfully implemented a few process changes you might consider taking on some of those that you put on the "For Future Consideration" list.

Here's another thought. If you can quantify the savings due to any of your successful process innovations, you might see if that money could be put towards one of the projects you wanted to take on that required a financial investment that was outside your company's comfort range. You just must be astonished to see management's reactions. Don't be surprised if after you've had a few successful projects, you become known as the innovator in your organization and other departments start looking at you in a new light. **DIYAP**

About the Publisher

CRYSTALLUS, Inc. is a boutique publishing, training, and consulting company focused on accounts payable issues. It publishes:

⇒ ***The Accounts Payable Now & Tomorrow newsletter***—a monthly publication for those who work in and/or manage the day-to-day operations of the accounts payable function

⇒ ***e-AP News***, a free weekly news alert with tips, updates and news of new AP products

Request a sample copy of any of these publications by emailing publisher@ap-now.com

The organization also produces a robust schedule of:

- webinars
- e-Learning events
- special publications
- CDs and
- one-day events—both Accounts Payable and 1099.

Please note: Any of AP Now's webinars or all-day seminars can be customized for your staff. The sessions can be delivered live at your location or online via the Internet. Call 302 836 0540 to discuss your unique requirements.
Check www.ap-now.com for details.

About Mary S. Schaeffer

Editorial Director & Publisher CRYSTALLUS, Inc.

- Nationally recognized accounts payable expert and consultant
- Frequent speaker at seminars, conferences and online events
- Publisher and editorial director of the Accounts Payable Now & Tomorrow monthly newsletter
- Editor-at-Large CFO Publishing's Learning Pro: AP Edition
- Regular contributor to the AICPA's Corporate Finance Insider
- Creator of Institute of Financial Operations Accounts Payable Innovation Certificate program
- Writes a free weekly e-zine, e-AP News
- Author more than 15 business books published by John Wiley & Sons, MeGraw-Hill and CRYSTALLUS, Inc. including the Controller & CFO's Guide to Accounts Payable and Fraud in Accounts Payable: How to Prevent It
- M.B.A. Finance, NYU; B.S. Math, York College (CUNY)

Check www.ap-now.com for details.

Periodicals for all Professionals:

- Our monthly Accounts Payable Now & Tomorrow newsletter. (details at http://ap-now.com/subscribe.html)

- The DIY AP Consultant Handbook (details at http://ap-now.com/special.html)

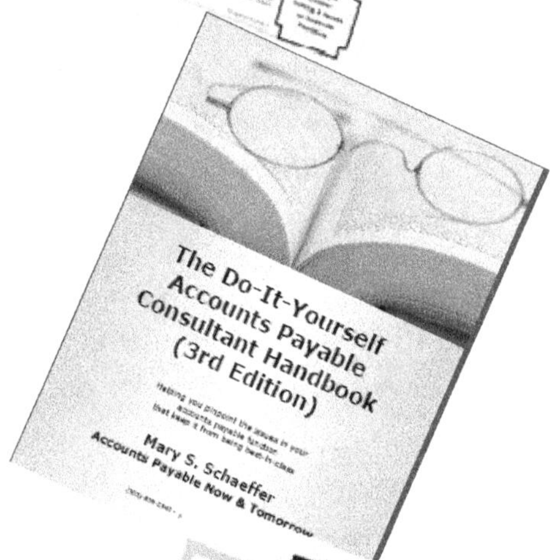

- A Short Guide to Creating A User-Friendly Accounts Payable Policy and Procedures Manual (details at http://ap

- For everyone, our free weekly e-AP News.

About the Accounts Payable Now & Tomorrow monthly newsletter

Accounts Payable Now & Tomorrow is a monthly publication delivered electronically in an Adobe format. It contains the most current advice from the trenches based on our reader surveys, interviews with some of the best practitioners, and the latest changes in all related specialty areas such as T&E, 1099s, sales and use tax, OFAC, VAT, electronic payment alternatives etc.. In addition to commentary from our editorial director, Mary S. Schaeffer, we feature a changing lineup of guest columnists, short book reviews, and the latest industry updates.

For additional information:
http://ap-now.com/aboutnl.html

About AP Now's webinars

We've got a dozen programs scheduled for 2012. Check back frequently. We'll be posting the details over the next few weeks. Better yet, sign up for our free weekly ezine. It's full of accounts payable tips and news as well as announcements of our upcoming programs.

Our one-hour audio conference/Webinars are designed to bring you succinct information about a discrete topic in a short period of time. We are proud to offer NASBA and IFO continuing education credits to Webinar participants. All Webinars take place at 2:00 p.m. EST (1:00 p.m. CST; noon MST; 11:00 a.m. PST) All our programs are sponsored by *Accounts Payable Now & Tomorrow*, a CRYSTALLUS, Inc. publication. All programs our 60-minutes are $189; 90-minute sessions are $239.

To see what topics we're currently featuring, visit
http://ap-now.com/accountspayablewebinars.html

CDs of all Sessions are available after the event. To see our current list of offerings visit:
http://ap-now.com/apcds.html

$149

- Accounts Payable Now & Tomorrow Newsletter (monthly)
- E-AP News weekly ezine (complimentary)
- Webinars/teleconferences
- Seminars
- CDs
- Special Reports
- Blog
- Consulting services
- Customized Training (including FCPA)
- Duplicate Payment Resource Center (complimentary)

www.ingramcontent.com/pod-product-compliance
Lightning Source LLC
LaVergne TN
LVHW082343200926
848481LV00012B/3435
9780615752143